AMERICAN FAN

AMERICAN FAN

SPORTS MANIA

AND THE CULTURE

THAT FEEDS IT

Dennis Perrin

SPIKE

AN AVON BOOK

AVON BOOKS, INC.
1350 Avenue of the Americas
New York, New York 10019

Copyright © 2000 by Dennis Perrin
Interior design by Kellan Peck
ISBN: 0-380-97732-X

Library of Congress Cataloging in Publication Data:
Perrin, Dennis.
    American fan : sports mania and the culture that feeds it / Dennis
Perrin—1st ed.
        p. cm.
    "An Avon book."
    Includes index.
    1. Sports—Anthropological aspects—United States.   2. Sports spec-
tators—United States.   3. Professional sports—United States.
I. Title.
        GV706.2.P47   2000   99-41417
        306.4'83'0973—dc21   CIP

First Spike Printing: January 2000

SPIKE TRADEMARK REG. U.S. PAT. OFF. AND IN OTHER COUNTRIES, MARCA REGISTRADA,
HECHO EN U.S.A.

Printed in the U.S.A.

FIRST EDITION

QPM   10   9   8   7   6   5   4   3   2   1

www.spikebooks.com

To God Shammgod
A Personal God

ACKNOWLEDGMENTS

I wish to thank my editor, Tom Dupree, for his support and insights, as well as his Avon Books colleagues, Lou Aronica, Joan Schulhafer, Kate Weaver and Kelly Notaras. My thanks also to Steve Gilbert, who was vital as a sounding board; my agent Mary Evans and her partner Tanya McKinnon; Tim Smith and Suzanne Simpson for their support; and, as always, Nancy Bauer, Katrina Bauer and Henry Perrin, for their love.

CONTENTS

Warm Up

"Kiss him, Freddie! *Hump* him!"

So said an older fan standing behind me at an Indiana Pacers home game. Time: circa 1971–72. League: the American Basketball Association. On the State Fair Coliseum floor, Pacers guard Freddie Lewis was playing tenacious man-to-man defense—against whom I do not recall. But I do remember Lewis's in-your-face style, which, along with the clutch shooting of Roger Brown, the inside game of Mel Daniels and Bob Netolicky, the power drives of Darnell Hillman and George McGinnis, the three-point accuracy of Billy Keller and the coaching of Bobby "Slick" Leonard, made the Pacers the most formidable and entertaining team in ABA history.

Since my father had season tickets (good seats near midcourt), I was privileged to see these giants as they captured three ABA crowns. I was also exposed to the screams and moans of Pacers fans, a knowledgeable, passionate crowd that moved singly but to my eyes never menacingly. It was in the ancient Coliseum where I first witnessed fan loyalty, fan betrayal, fan happiness, fan anger. It was also the place where I heard some of the most creative profanity of my young life. For a boy of twelve there was no finer combination: championship ball and men fashioning crude but sturdy epigrams with the words *fuck, shit,* and *goddam;* poetry to my ears, though I could never recreate the cadences for schoolmates who lacked access to this world but were fascinated by it all the same. Today, of course, kids twelve and under curse with the confidence and dexterity of seasoned orators. It is they, and not the older folk, who set the profane creative standard while watching, say, the NBA—assuming they are not bored by so dated a game.

I have been a sports fan forever. My father played football, which he loved (and still loves) with a fervor he shared for other major sports. My mother was equally fanatic about many of the same pastimes, and she remains, without doubt, the most loyal Yankees booster in central Indiana (poor Mom). Their passions inevitably became mine, yet I preferred the alternative leagues. There was, as I've said, the ABA with its garish red, white, and blue ball that was symbolic of the league's wide-open play. I also followed the American Football League and rooted for it in the premerger Super Bowl games. (I have fond memories of Curt Gowdy calling the "AFL Game of the Week"—Joe Namath's Jets against Daryl Lamonica's Raiders, or Len Dawson's Chiefs, or Bob Griese's Dolphins, or John Hadl's Chargers . . .) In time, however, the alternatives were consumed by the established leagues, and the alternatives that followed did not have the sizzle of the earlier upstarts.

The World Football League? I went along for the ride but found the team names more interesting than the players or the games: Philadelphia Bell, Birmingham Vulcans, Detroit Wheels, Chicago Fire (which became the Chicago Winds before dying out), Memphis Southmen (for whom Larry Csonka, Jim Kiick, and Paul Warfield bolted the Dolphins in 1975, and among whose fans was the soon-to-be-late Elvis), Charlotte Hornets, Honolulu Hawaiians, Southern California Sun, and the greatest team name of all time, the Shreveport Steamer. My one goal during the WFL's brief existence was to obtain an "official" Steamer T-shirt or any memorabilia that would announce my allegiance to a team that I'd never seen play. Little did I know at the time that the Steamer, like the other WFL franchises, was about to collapse. Had I been older, I might have flown to Shreveport to buy a jersey off the back of a desperate player, keeping one step ahead of the local sheriff whose job it probably was to arrest scavengers, take their money, fracture their skulls with a rifle butt, and dump them in a nearby swamp. In its final days, the WFL resembled the fall of Phnom Penh—not a good place to flash money and make last-minute deals.

The World Hockey Association? Like the WFL, there were colorful team names: Miami Screaming Eagles, Toronto Toros, Cincinnati Stingers, Quebec Nordiques. I was an Indianapolis Racers fan, my favorite player being defenseman Kim Clackson, whose left fist, a white blur when in action, often tenderized the face of the New England Whalers' Nick

Fitiou, Clackson's arch foe. So absorbed was I with Clackson that I overlooked a young Racers prospect who, after a few games and a few goals, was sold to the Edmonton Oilers—Wayne Gretzky. Had the Great One stayed in Indy, I later thought, perhaps the Racers would have entered the NHL with the four WHA teams that did. After all, one reason for this merger/expansion was to bring Gretzky into the old league, much in the same way that the NBA wanted Julius Erving and acquired four ABA teams to get him. But in reality the Racers were bankrupt and needed cash, which is why Gretzky (along with Peter Driscoll and Eddie Miro) went north. Since the WHA's demise in 1979, there has been only one serious attempt to create another pro alternative: the United States Football League in 1983. The USFL boasted some fine players, among them Jim Kelly (Houston Gamblers), Herschel Walker and Doug Flutie (New Jersey Generals), Sean Landeta and Bart Oates (Philadelphia Stars), all of whom moved on to the NFL. While it did slightly better than the WFL, the USFL lacked the suicidal flash of that doomed enterprise and it never coined a team name as beautiful and as timeless as the Shreveport Steamer.

Although I have written a book about sports, I do not claim to be a sportswriter. I say this because sportswriting is a wicked game itself; every columnist and hack seeks edges and angles to show that he alone understands a particular team's chemistry, a coach's mind-set, a player's motivation. They are an opinionated bunch who use shreds of fact to enhance or excuse various theories and predictions. (Political writers do this too, but believe theirs is a higher calling.)

Sportswriters are, as I explain later in the book, professional fans, and like most fans they view with a cold eye any stranger to their turf. I am indeed that stranger. But I'm also a fan, an amateur who keeps pace with the major leagues and whose happier moments are tied to classic games and outstanding individual plays. For years I have quietly observed our peculiar sports culture as it mutated into the corporate behemoth that towers over us. And like the middle-aged scientist in any Gamura movie you can name, I now point to the sky and yell at the beast, my words nearly in sync with the movement of my mouth.

For all the books written about sports, few have focused on the fans. There is Frederick Exeley's 1968 novel, *A Fan's Notes,* about a man obsessed with the New York Giants, in particular, Frank Gifford. Exeley's first-person account of an alcoholic who uses football as an emotional crutch has been hailed for its power. It is certainly of its time, the fanaticism displayed rather tame compared to the present drunken madness seen on Sunday fall afternoons. The book also deals with isolation, at least as it was felt in the days before cable when seasons ran fourteen games and the NFL was one league, not two conferences. Today's boozy fan who needs football to get him through the next drink can stick a satellite dish on his roof and, assuming he hasn't fallen to his death, watch multiple games on a multiscreen TV, his isolation buried in noise and endless highlights. And who attacked this current malaise? Why Mike Lupica did in *Mad As Hell,* a book—no, a call to action!—that alerted fans to the ongoing shell game being played at their expense by owners and players alike. Lupica makes some obvious points, but one wonders if the type of person he supposedly tried to reach actually read the thing. *Mad As Hell* seems, from this fan's perspective, a marketing effort to prove that millionaire Mike is on the side of the little guy. He's clearly disgusted by the excesses of modern sports, as well he should be. Yet Lupica remains among the elite sports reporters in the country.* *His* disgust has not altered his dealings with the pig culture he describes. He bitches, he whines, but in the end he feeds at the same trough where fan interests are routinely undermined.

A great book written about fans has nothing at all to do with the United States. *Among the Thugs* by Bill Buford is the ultimate nightmare volume on fan obsession and violence. Buford got inside the English football world and brilliantly captured its menace; the reader is with him in stands that shake with tribal fury, in pubs where the faithful load up on meat pies and ale, on the road between matches that resemble the "Dawn of Man" water hole scene in *2001*. He makes sociological points without resorting to sociology—no easy task. While reading *Thugs* I marveled at Buford's detachment. In a pack of howling, drinking men, I tend to lose my authorial distance and become as psychotic as the rest. It's a tic that I've never been able to shake and for the life of me I don't know where it originates. There's just something about mob behavior that lights my fuse and sets me off. This is why, at playoff time, friends keep me from attending deciding games. My conduct can be horrible, but I'm told I'd be at home in Yankee Stadium.

*Yet, as I show in Chapter 3, he is also in sportswriting's avant-garde.

In the following pages, I attempt to illustrate those areas where American sports fans affect the culture and how the wider culture in turn affects them. I touch on the familiar elements of American fandom: painted upper torsos, cheeseheads, bleacher bums and creatures, and the rest. These figures dot the landscape but do not define it; indeed, "colorful" fans serve as fringe on the edge of sports. They are used in league and network marketing as flattering if eccentric symbols of team loyalty and ballpark fun. They are ornaments that reflect attention away from the sporting world's true purpose: making team owners and their allies even fatter at public expense. With the exception of Green Bay, where Packers fans are team stockholders, most fans of major league franchises are bent over railings while owners act out the love scene from *Deliverance*—and then are asked for a donation afterward. Some fans resist such "attention," but many feel, with certain reservations, that they have no choice in the matter: Either give it up or see your team go away.

Degrading though it is, giving it up no longer guarantees that a team will remain in a fan's hometown. There are owners who fairly wheeze from the amount of pork they've ingested. They're so accustomed to screwing fans that they no longer bother zipping their flies, and in certain cases forgo wearing pants altogether. When they've had their fill of fan tail, they waddle off to a "friendlier" city where their special "needs" are met: a new stadium, more sky boxes, tax breaks so outrageous that even the IRS is rendered dumb. And of course there's the fresh supply of compliant fans, happy to be part of the big sports combine. Lines snake outside the new stadium, named after the corporation that made the highest bid, while inside, amid sturdy titanium railings, the owners rate the locals' ability to squeal.

Thankfully, a growing number of fans are getting wise to this routine. They still enjoy their favorite games but are willing to sacrifice pleasure in favor of principle. It was in this spirit that *American Fan* was written. Whenever sports commentators tell players and owners to resolve their financial differences and "get on with the season" for "the sake of the fans," I simply laugh. Let the bastards haggle over salary caps and free agency. Let them cry into their cell phones between rounds of golf. Let them plead their case to people who'll never see one-eightieth of 0.1 percent of the interest earned on a signing bonus no matter how long they live. I really don't care. In fact, I applaud strikes and lockouts. A periodic cleansing of sports toxins is vital to a healthy system. This is why I welcomed the baseball strike in 1994. As Bob Costas spoke of the season's death in somber tones and noted that there would be no World Series, I tossed Pop Secret in my mouth and drank Sapporo beer. When the strike ran into '95 and replacement players began spring training, my thoughts turned to the prospect of a replacement player All-Star Game and, yes, World Series. Regrettably, this never came to pass once the real major leaguers, appalled that the owners would field teams composed of plumbers and teachers, returned to work and eliminated the possibility of a Rockies/Brewers replacement Fall Classic.

American sports can be beautifully sordid, but there's

only so much one can set between covers. Here I focus primarily on the Big Three: pro football, baseball and basketball. Hockey, while popular at the amateur level, has never really captured a large domestic audience. (Indeed, during the NBA lockout in 1998, NHL fan attendance *dropped* in several cities.) Boxing and golf appear briefly, as does pro wrestling (the culture of which deserves a few volumes of its own). All sports boast elements worthy of discussion, but only with the Big Three does one get the full spectrum of our national insanity. I break everything down into four sections and in each try to nail the fan angle: Chapter 1, patriotism and religion; Chapter 2, race, violence, and drugs; Chapter 3, fans who become celebrities and celebrities who are outspoken fans; Chapter 4, the marketing of sports to consumers. At times the topics spill over from one chapter to the next, most notably the volatile subject of race. Alert readers will also notice that I deal almost exclusively with male sports and male fans. I do so for the simple reason that this is where the true lunacy lies. Women's games do not inspire the same aggression (unless I've missed some lesbian softball riot), and pro leagues like the WNBA have yet to permanently influence the culture, though the league's marketing wing is doing quite well. So I'll plead guilty up front to writing a sexist book and hope to even things out in my next project, *Heather's Two Mommies Are Liberty Fans.*

If we are to seriously explore what it means to be a fan in the present day, the definition of fandom must change to keep pace with the brutal expansion of sports itself. This requires a violent thrust into the belly of American sports, for it is there that we'll find answers to questions too obvious to be asked: i.e., Why is such emotion spent on overdeveloped strangers? Is said emotion organic or stirred by market forces? How drunk does one have to get before taking a swing at Charles Barkley? These and other, deeper queries will be addressed—ripped from the gut, as it were. In the words of a Taoist priest, "It is only through aggressive action that truth may be discerned." Or as my bartender is fond of saying when a team he has bet on loses or fails to cover the spread, "Everybody get the fuck out of my bar before I kick your sorry asses in the street! Go on! *Beat it!!*"

1

The First Refuge

In Dr. Johnson's famous dictionary, patriotism is defined as the last [refuge] of a scoundrel. With all due respect to an enlightened but inferior lexicographer, I beg to submit that it is the first.

—AMBROSE BIERCE

God is the immemorial refuge of the incompetent, the helpless, the miserable. They find not only sanctuary in His arms, but also a kind of superiority, soothing to their macerated egos: He will set them above their betters.

—H. L. MENCKEN

Aluminum whacks leather. Tiny infielders react. Shortstop and third baseman cross paths as the ball hits the dirt between them and skips into left field. Baserunner sees the winding arm of the third base coach, turns on the bag, and heads home. Left fielder, playing too deep, catches up to the ball, grabs it barehanded, and throws wildly to the plate. Catcher stares up through his mask; the ball flies overhead, slams the backstop fence, rattles the metal links. Runner easily scores, the game ends, and the poor left fielder, now inspecting his glasses, receives stares and sarcastic jibes as his team walks slowly to the bench.

Scenarios like this tug the heart. The purity of youth expressed through sport appeals to all—or should. Tales of sandlot glory, once plentiful in pulp fiction, radio serials, and film, have given way to transgressive themes. Some of the old tales resurface now and then—from *The Bad News*

Bears, where Walter Matthau guides a band of Little League misfits past its weaknesses to engage a superior team, to *The Mighty Ducks* trilogy, where Emilio Estevez guides a band of hockey misfits past its weaknesses and helps clear the ice for the ultimate marketing tie-in, an NHL team called the Mighty Ducks, a live-action product placement seeking Disney's first Stanley Cup. These and similar treatments, like *Little Giants* and *The Big Green,* which deal with football and soccer respectfully (but not *too* respectfully—more misfits), serve as reminders that sports are meant to be fun, character-building activities. As pro athletes command salaries large enough to choke the middle class, the allure of kids playing for kicks remains.

You see it on the faces of parents and relatives lining diamonds, football fields, and soccer fields: wide smiles, shouts of encouragement, applause for RBIs, touchdowns, and goals. Here the essence of sportsmanship is honored . . . until that missed tackle, blown steal, weak kick, after which the shouting becomes less encouraging. If a young player's relations are drawn to the action with any intensity, then pity the young player. It's a sight common to child leagues throughout the country. Parents driven by a competitive nature they cannot control oftentimes go crazy in the face of bad plays by their kids or bad calls by the officials. Profanities and put-downs are heard; threats made. Assault is also a possibility.

Ray Knight, the former Met and manager of the Reds, who in the spring of 1999 was coach of his daughter's softball team in Albany, Georgia, was charged with disorderly conduct after he punched another parent attending a game. The parent, Jimmy C. Smith, heckled Knight from the stands and the two met after the game to exchange pleasantries. "You couldn't play with the big boys and couldn't coach [in the majors], so you have to come here and coach a girls' softball team," said Smith to Knight, who then clipped Smith on the ear, causing a small cut. Each faced a small fine, but there were no reports of a rematch.

In the spring of 1998, the National Association of Sports Officials reported an increase in parents and coaches attacking officials, especially in Little League, and it began to offer assault insurance to its members. How inspiring it must be for kids to see adults strangle, stab, and shoot each other over perceived balks, balls called as strikes (and vice versa), and missed tags called as outs. Since background checks on potential Little League coaches are made only in select areas, a fair number of psychos, boozers, wife and child beaters can occupy benches and baselines, waiting for a call that hotwires their brains and sends them, pinwheel eyes aflame, onfield to right the wrongs they have suffered.

Of course not every Little League coach is nuts. Some are proud traditionalists. In an ABC documentary hosted by Peter Jennings, we see the coach of an all-star Little League team who's been handed a girl to play. She bats .500 and dreams of playing for the Yankees, but Coach hates this trend of mixing the sexes on the diamond. He is, in his own words, "absolutely sexist" (and no doubt "politically incorrect" as well), so the girl is occasionally used as a first base coach and nothing more. Coach is stern. "I would never tell my daughter that you're not allowed to play baseball. I wouldn't encourage her to play. I'd encourage her to be a cheerleader. I'd encourage her to be a ballerina . . ." Plainly the girl's parents have been derelict in her upbringing. If they heed Coach's advice, their daughter could instead lead the charmed life of Gelsey Kirkland. But Little League traditionalism is hardly limited to sex. Tribe matters too, and no finer barometer gauges this feeling than does the Little League World Series, played annually in Williamsport, Pennsylvania.

The series began in 1947. It was a modest regional affair. Teams from across the Keystone State and neighboring New Jersey played for the "World" title, which, in this outing, was subjective in the extreme. The following year saw other teams from other states compete, making the series a national event. In 1957 the series expanded to include a team from Mexico, which promptly won the title and then again in 1958. From here international youth were involved in what was truly now a World Series. In 1964 the first Asian team appeared representing Japan and soon the gongs of distant temples rattled American ears. From 1967 to 1999, teams from either Japan, Taiwan, or South Korea won the series twenty-three times; seven of the remaining nine titles were won by the United States, the other two by Latin American teams. From '67 to '74, the Far East lost once, in 1970. Then in 1975, the series was comprised solely of U.S. teams and was won by a team from Lakewood, New Jersey, later dubbed "Champions for Life" by *The New York Times*. The next year the Asians returned to Williamsport and again conquered the decadent West, with Taiwan winning four of the five subsequent titles.

Asian domination of "our" boys playing "our" game irritated many patriots, and there was some talk of limiting or eliminating Far Eastern teams from the series. Rumors flew that the Taiwanese sent squads comprised of older teens or adult midgets passing as boys. Who knew the depth of Yellow deception? After another victory in 1996, however, the Taiwan express hit a wall. It was discovered that many of the leagues on the island took players from schools with three times as many pupils as the total allowed under Little League World Series rules. So Taiwan was barred from sending a team to Williamsport in 1997 (though they could reapply the following year). But despite the ban there was no returning to 1947. Save for the 1975 Series, which doubtless warmed isolationist hearts, the United States could not avoid the better foreign teams. Ultimately it was decided that there be two series brackets: one international and one domestic. That way a U.S. team was guaranteed a place in the championship game, where with luck and the grace of a Christian God, victory would be secured. Even with this leg-up, however, American ass continually got whipped.

There were exceptions. U.S. West won the series in 1992 and '93. In 1998 the country, or at least the Eastern coast of it, went crazy over a plucky group of kids from Toms River, New Jersey, who played not only the best ball of their young lives, but also the role of American David to Japan's supposed Goliath. Many "win or lose, they're still winners" remarks were made before the championship game—a clear indication that most thought the U.S. team doomed. But Toms River was equal to the Japanese squad, and the game itself was a see-saw battle of home runs and aggressive base-running. Jersey outlasted Japan, 12–9, and for a brief moment the Garden State, so often ridiculed, became a symbol of national pride. Such was the extra weight put on the American kids. It wasn't enough that Toms River had a fine, resourceful team; they had to be "America's Team" as well. As the game progressed, the inevitable "U.S.A.! U.S.A.!" chant was heard, a sad but essential part of the tribal spirit. The beauty of individual and team play was reduced to a patriotic crack hit with the kids used as pipes.

Since Americans do not face foreign competition until the final game, the primary emotion seen throughout the series is regionalist in origin: U.S. East against U.S. West, and so on. Here regional tribalism is most acute, though it's the adults in the stands who bray loudest. The eleven- and twelve-year-old boys have yet to fully feel the tribal pulse; they simply play baseball because it is a fun game to play. By the time they reach high school, the pulse beats in them like drums in a speed metal band. Testosterone fuels a large portion of this, but the genital rush is meaningless unless someone shows the boys how best to channel it. Enter those parents, teachers, and coaches eager to steer teen jocks in "positive" directions. Pride in one's school, loyalty to one's community, and dedication to the glory of both serve as the bedrock of regional tribal rites. And there, amid the chanting and shaking of fists, stand authority figures confident in their wisdom and thrilled to see fine young men putting all that energy to good use.

This primitive order survives in rural and suburban areas where, despite (or perhaps because of) satellite TV and the World Wide Web, life remains for most an isolated, insular affair. Urban high schools have their share of rallies and related expressions of pep, but city kids are connected to so many things that the concept of regionalism—much less school spirit—is faint. This is especially true in schools where students must dodge falling concrete and random gunfire. To what does one swear allegiance? Although some rural and suburban schools share similar problems, including those roving tribes known as gangs, they nevertheless represent something more than just classrooms and gyms. For many in a small community, the high school symbolizes their collective identity, which, in certain cases, mutates into collective insanity.

Consider Texas. The Lone Star obsession with high school football, celebrated by many, baffles rational folk, including those who enjoy the game. But deep in the heart, darker values reign. One's connection to a small-town team (or to even some of the larger ones) is forged in blood and Friday night is Black Mass. The sound of competing cheering sections, rich in Texan drawls and screams, is considerably more violent than the action on-field. At times it resembles *Lord of the Flies* as staged by the followers of Sade. Indeed, Texas fan behavior is so intense and terrifying that players have feigned injuries so they may leave the game and hide in the locker room, while some simply forfeit and run, convinced that their lives are in danger.

As crazed as Texas football fans can be, their obsessions are minor when compared to Hoosier "hysteria." In Indiana, basketball tribalism is particularly extreme. So manic are the fans that one may view them as insects at feast. Yet like a colony of ants dismembering a beetle in their path, there is a rough beauty in Hoosier fan behavior: To sit in a crowded small-town gym as the boys run the floor is to experience the insect collective at fever pitch. The gym becomes a bright nest where vibration and scent guide one through the four quarters. It is not a feeling that is easily shrugged off; and should the game go to overtime, the conscious mind fades and it is hours before one's mammal senses return.

In Indiana the clichés are true. The game not only means something, it usually is *everything*. This frenzied devotion to one's team was partially captured in the cornfield-realist film, *Hoosiers*. A warm retelling of the Milan tale, wherein a tiny school of hicks wins the 1954 Indiana state championship with a buzzer-beating shot (though Milan won its championship in 1952), *Hoosiers* shows what basketball means to those for whom identity and town are synonymous. The emotion the film taps into is quite real and moving in its own way, though it is cranked up to a mystical level in the scene where Dennis Hopper is cleansed of alcoholism thanks to the healing powers of a tournament victory.* Still, *Hoosiers* gives us a glimpse of the passion that made Indiana famous, and the

---

*Word is that originally Hopper's character, in the grip of detox hallucinations, was to be haunted by the ghosts of dead Globetrotters who perform all their gags, including the bucket of confetti, until Hopper is cured. But this ethereal rendition of "Sweet Georgia Brown" did not enhance the scene and was dropped.

film is usually cited as Exhibit A whenever the subject of basketball fanaticism is raised.

Unlike Texas football fans who practice their rituals out-doors, Hoosier fanatics hone their techniques in basements and barns. Strange tales have traveled the Farm Belt, from severed pig heads nailed to backboards to dogs pitted against each other in savage games of one-on-one. Indiana winter is a cold lonely time when the minds of committed fans are reduced to all manner of depravity. Occasionally, the de-praved turn from animals to people. In a January 1998 game between Martinsville and Bloomington North, there were re-ports that a Martinsville fan uttered racial slurs in the direc-tion of a North player, Kueth Duany, after he was elbowed in the gut and promptly vomited. "That nigger's spitting on the floor!" the person allegedly yelled. "Get his ass off the floor!" Other charges made by North fans and Duany's team-mates reinforced the image of a Klan mob in the stands. Mar-tinsville won the game in overtime, 69–66. Bloomington's fan buses needed a police escort to escape what became a nasty situation.

Martinsville is a small town just south of Indianapolis. Its private basketball rituals are unknown, but publicly its citizens are zealots of the traditional Hoosier stripe. Larry Bird owns a car dealership on the outskirts of town. The high school's gym is named after the great John Wooden, a native son. Backboards and rims are as prevalent as grass. In summer the main playground is choked with pickup games. And of course the town solidly, passionately supports its basketball teams, boys as well as girls (the latter state champions in '97 and '98). As is often the case in Indiana, the town's love of its teams verges on lunacy; and when mixed with a far-right view of the world that is born of Caucasian angst, tribal drums and chants are heard with regularity. Martinsville residents say this is simple community pride and they resent the racist label. But the town has been down this trail before. *ESPN Magazine* noted that in 1994, "members of one Martinsville middle school football team painted their faces black and taunted their Bloomington opponents. And in 1996, players on the Columbus Middle School football team accused Martinsville players of using racial slurs on the field."

Bloomington North boasts the kind of diversity that inspires such behavior. Its basketball team, that year the defending state champs, had on its roster players from the Sudan, the Philippines, and Indonesia. Bloomington too is a small town, but a college town, and this means race-mixing, faggotry, liberalism, and related crimes against nature. No doubt the Martinsville faithful cringe at the mere thought of it all; so it would be no surprise if a few of them went racial when Bloomington North appeared on their home court and when Kueth Duany, a gen-u-wine Aff-ree-cun, puked on their floor.

In a letter to the Martinsville *Daily Reporter,* one local reader wrote, "Racial slurs are only words and words cannot hurt unless you let them. I'm sure young people who suffered the supposed racial slurs will grow up with much worse things being said to them." (Especially if they linger in Martinsville after dark.) But this libertarian defense of the town and its citizens was either not heard by or did not dissuade the Indiana High School Athletic Association from placing Martinsville on probation. In addition, the boys team received a year's ban on all home games. The final insult came later that season when Martinsville lost to Bloomington North in the state tournament. Left to lick their wounds and curse their hard luck, team supporters watched videotapes of earlier games in an effort to dull the pain. Local youths played endless games—perhaps well into the night as the flames from a nearby cross illuminated rims and tattered nets—and no doubt dreamed of leading their home team back to grace as parents and friends cheered, white confetti fell, and the public address system boomed a hearty "Yeeeeee Haw!" from its speakers.

Let us not dwell on Martinsville, for there are many small towns in many states that use local teams to express collective pride and fear. And as noted earlier, tribalism is scarcely confined to regions. Its grandest form, patriotism, transcends intra-county rivalries by way of mystical appeal. Unfurl the Stars and Stripes and for many independent thought fades. Conditioning has much to do with this, of course, but a deeper need is met: The tribe is not only powerful and large, it is touched by divinity as well. Few riptides have this kind of pull, which is why politicians and ministers of various faiths exploit it without shame. Worse still, the majority allow them to do so.

It is surprising how late patriotic rituals were officially brought into sports, primarily the national pastime. From its days in distant fields to its early urban period, baseball was covered in American flags and its fans sang nativist songs. But it wasn't until 1918 after the United States had joined the slaughter in Europe that these shows of pride converged. In the seventh-inning stretch in the first game of that year's World Series, "The Star-Spangled Banner" was played. The Comiskey Park crowd of Cubs and Red Sox fans rose and sang as one. Americanism ruled. Everything German had been demonized; free speech was all but outlawed thanks to the Espionage Act; patriots ran riot through much of the culture, including the World Series. After that initial rendition, "The Star-Spangled Banner" was soon adopted as baseball's anthem, some thirteen years before it went national.

Days of spontaneous expression were past. Each game began with the "Banner"; then one was free to root for his team. Though no law was passed that made the ritual compulsory, only a brave few dared remained seated while the majority stood at attention, hands over hearts, throats in full cry. For so conceptual a game, it might seem odd that baseball lent itself to such regimentation. But the mystical force of patriotism can—and does—overtake the most passive of pursuits; and if there is military conflict overseas, mysticism gives way to direct action, especially in the more aggressive American games.

Take what was cleverly called "The Gulf War." In this 1991 made-for-TV miniseries, American pal Saddam Hussein succumbs to lycanthropy and becomes, overnight, "An Iraqi Werewolf in Kuwait." American troops are dispatched to tame this wild beast, while at home citizens wrap themselves in ribbons and flags and watch the "war" as they would an episode of "Cops." Athletes do their part. College basketball teams have American flags sewn onto their jerseys (a respectful distance from the Nike swoosh, of course), and players in the NFL stick flag decals on their helmets. Cut to: Tampa, Florida, January 27, 1991. Super Bowl Sunday. New York Giants versus Buffalo Bills. Some 70,000 fans are given tiny American flags. Whitney Houston, in a cameo appearance, lip-syncs the national anthem at midfield. The fans are as quiet as an Iraqi tomb. Then, their cue: ". . . and the home . . . of the . . . *brave!"* Flags are raised and vigorously waved. Fighter jets streak overhead. The goal posts sway in their wake. The stands rumble with emotion. Shirts are soaked with drool and beer.

The excitement spills onto the field. Every open-field tackle reminds fans of cruise missiles striking Baghdad; every completed pass a sortie knocking out a water purification plant. It is a Super Bowl with meaning—and closely played. The Bills are favored, but the Giants hold a one-point lead. The game is decided on the final play as Bills kicker Scott Norwood just misses the winning field goal, bringing victory instead to the Giants. Indeed, the game proves more competitive than "The Gulf War" itself, a splendid plot twist that makes the miniseries a critical and commercial triumph.

For fans of football and war, there was no better time. Even the postseason turkey shoot, where retreating Iraqi conscripts were chopped into burger, then charred, could not sate the appetites of those Americans who revel in lopsided displays of national might. Fortunately, they were served an extra helping the following year in Barcelona, Spain. There a group of NBA All-Stars called the Dream Team served notice to the world: No longer would Americans abide the mistreatment of their college boys by foreign basketball players. From this Olympiad on, only the true masters of the game would represent the country that invented the game; and in 1992 this meant Michael Jordan, Charles Barkley, John Stockton, David Robinson, Karl Malone, Patrick Ewing, as well as Larry Bird with his bad back and the HIV-positive Magic Johnson—both of whom, in their respective conditions, were superior to the other international players assembled. The Dream Team buried every squad it faced, smirking and cackling at the pathetic losers before it. It was a tournament of keep-away, like a gang of cocky thirteen-year-olds toying with children in a playground. American fans watched and howled along at home, basking in national honor.

Fan reaction to the Dream Team can be traced to the 1984 Summer Games in Los Angeles. There beneath Reagan's full moon and minus competition from the Soviet Bloc, Americans foamed with patriotic zeal. "U.S.A.! U.S.A.!" became mantra, having four years earlier in Lake Placid been a spontaneous, if crude, expression of national pride when the U.S. hockey team won the gold. But in 1984 spontaneity was left to those foolish enough to resist the prevailing mood. Who can forget that lovely display during the women's gymnastics competition when Americans screamed at the judges to give Mary Lou Retton high scores? Or when ABC's Jim Lampley proudly claimed to be jingoistic on a network whose Olympic coverage was just that? It became so shameless that a few natives recoiled, including a writer from *The Boston Globe*, Leigh Montville, who noted that the landscape was decidedly noninternational. "All I can see is American flags. Everywhere. On shirts. On hats. On banners. On the flagpoles." These were, he wrote, "America's games. No one else seems to matter."

Subsequent Olympiads have been (so far) less extremist in tone. The 1996 Games in Atlanta were a Teletubby hugfest compared to Los Angeles—save for the terror bombing, of course—and this was reflected in NBC's coverage that year. The Barcelona Games in 1992 played up the internationalist spirit, disrupted by the Dream Team and its toadies. So detached from the proceedings were Michael Jordan and crew that they refused to stay in the Olympic Village with the other competitors. Their presence in Barcelona was strictly promotional, both for the NBA and the companies that employed them as symbols. While the folks at home took pride in smashing inferior teams, the Dreamers were thinking in endorsement terms. In fact, Jordan wished to receive the gold medal while wearing the Nike swoosh. How confused His Airness must have been by requests that he not be so crass on the victory stand. *Why the fuss?* he certainly thought. In America this is not only accepted but celebrated and therefore correct. The passions of '84, when young Jordan first won gold, made possible the cool mindset of '92, when sage Jordan cashed in: marketing—nationalism with a bold new taste!

One wonders how MJ would have handled Mexico City in 1968. Now there was an Olympiad! Political statements made by American athletes against a backdrop of repression and mass murder—and this in the Mexican capital alone. Other events affected the tenor of those Games: Vietnam, Czechoslovakia, the assassinations of Martin Luther King, Jr., and Robert Kennedy, urban rioting in the U.S. and parts of Europe, the wounding of Andy Warhol, NBC's cancellation of "The Monkees," Jean Shrimpton vs. Twiggy, the Exploding Plastic Inevitable . . . But it was the black athlete, moving from Negro to Afro-American, who truly set the dissident mood. UCLA phenom Lew Alcindor, the premier player in college basketball next to Houston's Elvin Hayes, refused to join the Olympic team to protest the treatment of his brethren. Sprinters Tommie Smith and John Carlos did go to Mexico City, split a gold and bronze medal between them in the 200-meter finals, and then on the victory stand raised their black-gloved fists to the national anthem. This relatively passive act* turned red the eyes of the U.S. Olympic Committee. Smith and Carlos could have yelled "Fuck Whitey!" while urinating on the stand for the punishment they received: suspension from the team, banishment from the Olympic Village, and the forfeiture of their medals. For those Americans offended by the pair, they surely were calmed by George

*This incident was followed by a near-repeat performance by the winners of the 400-meter finals: Lee Evans, Larry James, and Ron Freeman. The three Americans mounted the victory stand wearing black berets and all raised their fists in salute. But once the national anthem began, the berets were removed and the hands, unclenched, were lowered to the runners' sides. None were disciplined.

Foreman's waving of the flag after he won the gold medal in boxing. The future heavyweight champ and infomercial star showed that not every Negro in Mexico City had dashikis on the brain.

But it was a gold medal champion from the 1960 Rome Games who ultimately tried the patriotic temper. In 1967 Muhammad Ali refused induction into the armed forces. He said that his interests were not threatened by Vietnamese nationalism and he framed his decision poetically: "No Vietcong ever called me nigger." He did not follow Lyndon Johnson but the Honorable Elijah Muhammad and so would not fight the white devil's war. Most American sportswriters, hungry for Asian blood, charged Ali with treason—one exception being Howard Cossell, who was also the first to respect Ali's shedding of Cassius Clay (unlike Ernie Terrell, whom Ali beat senseless while asking, *"Uncle Tom! What's my name?!"*). Ali was stripped of his heavyweight crown and driven from the sport he energized with ego, speed, and humor. Yet despite his dissidence and practice of a strange brand of Islam (did he really buy that fable about the evil black scientist Yacub?), Ali remained popular among many whites. What other black man with fists as fast and pride as brash as Ali's could maintain such devotion? Kareem Abdul-Jabbar, née Lew Alcindor, explained it best in the April 1998 issue of *GQ:*

You never felt fear. He could walk up to somebody's door at 3 A.M. and say, "I have a flat tire." And if they looked out the door, they'd say, "Hey, that's Mu-

hammad Ali," and they would come outside. Ali is
that familiar, but in a remarkable way.

Also, Ali opposed a war that grew unpopular by the day.
He stuck to his position regardless of cost and this hit a nerve
among those watching. In time he would twice win back his
title, retire, and become an elder, if ailing, statesman. His
stand in 1967 faded to nostalgia as subsequent stars like Michael Jordan played to the crowd and did nothing to rock
the endorsement boat. Indeed, by the time Jordan and other
mass-market jocks settled in for extended paydays, stands
that echoed Ali's were viewed with hostility and rage.* Take
the case of former Denver Nuggets point guard Mahmoud
Abdul-Rauf. During the 1995–96 NBA season, Abdul-Rauf
(slave name: Chris Jackson) led the Nuggets in scoring and
was regarded as one of the better points in the league. As
the season progressed, members of the press noticed that he
was always absent during "The Star-Spangled Banner."
Abdul-Rauf, whose name means "Elegant and Praiseworthy,
Servant of the Most Kind," felt it was his Muslim duty to
not honor a symbol of, in his words, "oppression and tyr-
anny." He would either come late to the court or sit on the
bench until the song's end. He did this quietly, made no
proclamations. He didn't need to: The press was happy to
shatter his silence.

The predictable occurred. NBA commandant David Stern

---

*Of course Ali was not above hawking consumer goods. Who can forget
his ode to a popular cologne of the 1970s? "Float like a butterfly/Sting like
a bee/The sweet smell of Brut/And the punch of Ali."

placed Abdul-Rauf on indefinite suspension.* He was not allowed to return until he praised Old Glory in full view of the league and its paying customers. Abdul-Rauf held out for three days, missed one game (which cost him over thirty grand), then finally acquiesced. "I'll stand," he said. "I will offer a prayer, my own prayer, for those who are suffering—Muslim, Caucasian, African American, Asian, or whoever is in that position, whoever is experiencing difficulty. This is what I cry out for." The notion of U.S. complicity with terror and oppression is science fiction to defenders of the faith, thus Abdul-Rauf was vilified from coast to coast. But the real fun took place on March 15, 1996, the night he returned to his team. The Nuggets were in Chicago to play the Bulls. With the opening notes of the anthem, the fan barrage began. An over-sized American flag was held just to Abdul-Rauf's left; placards were waved, insults shouted. It was a lesson in mob behavior hopefully absorbed by the children present. What better way to honor freedom than to harass someone who has a minority opinion and virtually no power to enforce it? Through it all, Abdul-Rauf remained silent, composed. During the game, he was booed whenever he touched the ball, while Citizen Rodman received cheers as he smirked and strutted between rebounds, and MJ pondered stock options during the timeouts.

The anti-American stigma stayed with Abdul-Rauf for the

---

*Stern was quite the patriot, not only in the Abdul-Rauf matter but later in the Great Lockout of '98. When it became obvious that NBA players would boycott the world championships in Athens that year, Stern, coonskin cap in place, said, "If the individual players decide to trash their country, that's going to be their decision." Translation: It is treason to not help promote the NBA in European markets. Not even the loyal Michael Jordan was swayed by this argument.

rest of that season. He quietly weathered verbal abuse and went about his job. He was then sent to NBA Siberia, the Sacramento Kings,* where for nearly two seasons he plied his trade until a corneal ulcer in his left eye forced him to the sidelines. The Kings made it clear that they had no further use for Abdul-Rauf, regardless of recovery. Once Sacramento took a pass, his NBA days were over. Abdul-Rauf saw the writing on the locker room wall: LOVE IT OR LEAVE IT. So he left to play ball in that Kurdish paradise, Turkey.

Was Abdul-Rauf's conduct that egregious? In the land of the free, yes. At the time of his suspension, there was much legal talk about his flouting the NBA rule concerning participation in the anthem ceremony. He was expected to follow company orders. But the league ignored his silent act of conscience—until it became a media issue. This forced Stern's hand. After all, the NBA is a Disney spectacle; when a mascot disturbs the tourists' sense of fantasy and fun, he is driven from the Magic Kingdom and forced to work at Midnight Expressland. Though his numbers fell while in Sacramento, Abdul-Rauf was still an NBA-caliber guard. But his image ruffled too many fans who prefer endless fast breaks capped with screams of triumph. Who the fuck cares about the "oppressed"?

Mahmoud Abdul-Rauf's problem was that he was not Muhammad Ali. For one thing, he lacked the global fame of the three-time heavyweight champ—a major setback when

---

*This before the Kings enjoyed a minor renaissance with the additions of Chris Webber and Jason "White Chocolate" Williams. The new Siberia is currently split between the Grizzlies and, of course, the Clippers.

flouting tribal rites. But perhaps more damaging, Abdul-Rauf never raised a public stink about his rights or his beliefs. He failed to adopt grandstand tactics and this proved a crucial error. Once Cassius Clay became Muhammad Ali, he let the crackers *know it.* He taunted them as he did Terrell, Floyd Patterson, and Sonny Liston; called them devils; spat on their idols; told them Jesus Christ was *black.* When he resisted the draft, he was bold, unrepentant, and again bashed white America for good measure. Ali vilified beautifully. His carnival barker style, part of the American rhetorical tradition, riveted people regardless of color. Abdul-Rauf was far too modest and withdrawn to connect with the public and so paid the price. The comedienne Roseanne caught similar heat for her take on the anthem in 1990. She sang deliberately off-key, scratched her crotch, and spit in the dirt as thousands of Padres fans in Jack Murphy Stadium riddled her with boos. She meant it as a joke; they saw it as sacrilege. But her persona was such that eventually the gag was forgotten. Roseanne, like Ali, was showfolk, unlike Abdul-Rauf, whose seriousness did him in.

If Abdul-Rauf's religion told him to snub Old Glory, then most Americans feel his religion is wrong. However, religion itself is not unwelcome in sports; just those strange, exotic faiths where Jesus is banished from the main stage or is recast as an African warrior-prince twirling a crucifix spear. The God who loves American sports is a Christian God, of that there is little doubt, and the number of athletes and fans who praise Jesus and look to Him for inspiration grows hourly. The days of quaint believers wearing multicolor Afro wigs and holding JOHN 3:16 signs in camera shot have more or less ended. The near future belongs to aggressive evangelicals and their barbarous concept of God's love and glory—the Lord as enlightened tyrannosaur chasing sinners through the jungles of evil. In stadium pockets nationwide, body-painted Christians belt out, in fluctuating grunts and shouts, not only John 3:16:

> *For GOD so loved the world that he gave his ONE and ONLY BEGOTTEN SON, that whoever believes in HIM shall not PERISH but have ETERNAL LIFE . . .*

but also John 3:18, without which 3:16 is mere liberal sentiment:

> *Whoever BELIEVES in HIM is NOT condemned, but whoever does NOT BELIEVE stands CONDEMNED already because he has NOT BELIEVED in the name of GOD'S ONE AND ONLY SON.*

From here a believer can go pretty much anywhere he or she prefers, so long as connection is maintained. Indeed, Christianity is one of the more flexible faiths, which (partly) explains its ongoing appeal. Sects form and split like amoebas and each, of course, knows Christ better than the others. Practices differ: Some sing folk songs, some wave snakes, some speak in tongues, some simply hold meetings. But scratch certain Christians and the odds are good you'll be savaged in return. This Dennis Rodman learned during the

36

1997 NBA Finals. After a sluggish performance in Game 3 against the Jazz in Salt Lake City, Rodman told reporters, "It's difficult to get in sync because of all the asshole Mormons out here. And you can quote me on that." The reporters did and an uproar ensued. Rodman refused to apologize, however; he repeated his description of Mormons, then added, "Maybe I don't know some of the Mormon people. The Mormon people don't like me either, right? That's a given, right? So what the hell." The NAACP called for a public apology, and the Anti-Defamation League cried "hate speech" and demanded that the NBA "take action." Rodman was eventually fined $50,000 for his remarks, though from the ADL's tone it would seem nothing less than an old-fashioned stoning would suffice. From the Mormon Church there was little comment. The Associated Press interviewed a Mormon-in-the-street, who said simply, "Some people will take offense, but we're used to it because we've been persecuted ever since the church was founded in 1830." It is true that Mormons have received hostility—primarily from rival Christian sects intent on upturning the Mormon faith itself. In June 1998 the Southern Baptists held a three-day convention in Salt Lake City to save the followers of "a counterfeit Christianity," as one minister put it. The Baptists were (and remain) much nastier to the Mormons than was Rodman the year before. No matter. Rodman was an easier target and so was singled out. Yet as bizarre as Rodman appeared to be (at least to conservative eyes), the brilliant rebounder and psychological terrorist paled when compared to Mormon lore. The Church of Jesus Christ of Latter-day Saints was founded by Joseph Smith in upstate New York after he was visited by the angel Moroni, who showed Smith the light. This visitation came centuries after the pre-crucified Jesus had appeared and ministered to Indian tribes in North and South America. (Some Mormons believe that God oversaw Smith's conversion from His home near the planet Kolob, where He lives with countless wives and spirit children, some of whom are sent to Earth to be tested in human form.) As do most Christian sects, Mormons believe that theirs is the one true faith. They also believe in baptizing the dead as a way to bolster their ranks.

Another element of Mormonism, besides the still-practiced (by some) art of polygamy, is the belief in white supremacy. In the Mormon text *Pearl of Great Price,* those who exhibit "the mark of Cain," which, for those confused, is a "flat nose and dark skin," are "inferior to the white race" and thus not in God's sight. Is this why many black NBA players consider Utah fans to be among the most abusive in the league? And while Rodman has inspired, indeed welcomed, derision from fans when on the road, did Jazz boosters shout that extra epithet that led him to call them "asshole Mormons"? Whatever the reasons, the sad part of this episode was the attack on Rodman for expressing his opinion, one that is no more nor less valid than the supernatural or racist claims made by Mormons themselves. Mormonism, like all religions, is a philosophy. No one is born believing its tenets; they must be taught and/or indoctrinated in the faith. It is therefore subject to scrutiny, even derision, which is, at least in theory, constitutionally protected speech—unless you happen to play in the NBA. There you'll be fined for impure thoughts while interest groups applaud. It's a good thing Mark Twain never played pro ball. He would be suspended for life and his book *Roughing It* banned by the offended once they crossed this passage: "The Mormon bible is rather stupid and tiresome to read . . . The book is a curiosity to me, it is such a pretentious affair, and yet so 'slow,' so sleepy; such an insipid mess of inspiration."

Unfortunately, Rodman lacked Twain's knowledge and wit. His anti-Mormon crack was nonreligious in character. As Bulls coach Phil Jackson explained at the time, Rodman thought a "Mormon" was someone who lived in Utah, a nickname like "Buckeye" or "Hoosier." Jackson, on the other hand, understood well the term. After all, he was a spiritual man himself, a "Zen Christian" with a Native mystic edge. Were Jackson, say, Cotton Fitzsimmons, his philosophy would have been ridiculed by sportswriters and commentators who dare not mock traditional Christian sects. But Jackson had Michael Jordan and Scottie Pippen, the linchpins of six championship teams. This made him immune to sarcasm (everybody loves a winner), and the worst tag he got was "Big Chief Triangle" for his devotion to the triangle offense. But he was equally devoted to meditative techniques, which, as he explained to the readers of *ESPN The Magazine,* helped to ease his team's tensions:

All the players sit in a group and try to do it. Some go willingly, some don't . . . Ten minutes at the most. Eyes slightly open, sitting in chairs. Lights down a

little. You'd like to hear your heart beat, but not con-
centrate on it . . . It's stress management."

Suffice it to say, Jackson's applied philosophy has
worked well for his teams. However, he is human and has
often failed Lao-tzu's test: "He who knows does not speak.
He who speaks does not know." At times he ignored Sun
Tzu's advice in *The Art of War:* "Be extremely subtle, even
to the point of formlessness. Be extremely mysterious, even
to the point of soundlessness. Thereby you can be the director of the opponent's fate." Jackson spoke and sounded off
quite a lot. Whenever his sacred Bulls lost, Jackson raised
his voice in a non-Zen whine: it was the officiating; the other
team got away with murder; our beautiful, elegant players
were mugged by lesser thugs; and so on. During the 1998
Eastern Conference Finals against the Indiana Pacers, Jackson's whine cracked backboards and sent ballboys to the
floor, wincing. For not only were the Bulls nearly eliminated
by the resilient Pacers, Jackson himself stared into the face
of a true Zen master: Larry Bird.

"The Hick from French Lick" emerged that year as the
Pacer priest. Impassive, quiet, the calm within storms, Bird
did what Jackson professed to do. He spoke only when he
felt it necessary, oftentimes with a wry, ironical tone befitting
a samurai who spares inferiors the kiss of his blade. His
expression remained constant no matter the situation. (When
Reggie Miller broke free of Jordan to sink a game-winning
jumper, everyone on the Pacers bench leapt to cheer—except
Bird. To him, Miller performed as expected. The arrow hit

the bull's-eye and that was that.) Not that Bird was always thus. During his prime with the Celtics, Bird was *the* premier trash talker of the league. He took so many players to school that many of them now hold reunions. His lessons were brief and rough and few forgot what they learned. Once his warrior days ended, Bird relinquished his sword and moved serenely to the next level, a place Phil Jackson had claimed as his own.

Buddhism, however fashionable in certain circles (how soon before the Dalai Lama sits courtside at the Staples Center?), is too ethereal for many Americans to grasp. Islam is okay, so long as the Muslim in question kneels to Mecca in private and keeps his odd customs from affecting his game. (If Hakeem Olaijuwan averages at least twenty-points during his Ramadan fast, all is well.) Judaism is as strange to the mass as is Zen, though there have been some fine Jewish pro athletes like Dolph Schayes, Sandy Koufax, and Hank Greenberg. But to the majority, nothing beats Jesus nailed to a cross. That crown of thorns, that blood trickling from palms and feet, that look of celestial anguish—what better image to inspire players and coaches to victory? If Jesus can take that kind of punishment, what's a broken rib or collarbone, a cracked femur, torn cartilage? By ignoring mortal pain and focusing on the promise of eternal life, jocks enter an injury-free world where touchdown drives, three-point shots, grand slams and tie-breaking goals are commonplace. The Lord is loyal to those who are loyal to Him, hence the surge in clubhouse chapels, on-field prayer circles, and winning players who grunt into microphones, "I want to thank my savior

Jesus Christ for this victory . . ." It is rare to hear a postgame, non-Christian shout out to the Creator, but the Knicks' Larry Johnson, after completing a four-point play to beat the Pacers in Game Three of the 1999 Eastern Conference Finals, did just that, telling NBC's Jim Gray over and over how Allah blessed LJ's winning trivector in crunch time.

Bathed in divine light, the athlete may act without fear. Before the 1997 Super Bowl, the Packers' Desmond Howard knelt in prayer and centered on the task ahead. Green Bay buried the Patriots early; Howard showed the spirit of the Lord was in him as he strutted and preened for the crowd, then taunted the New England bench well after the outcome was decided. The Packers were blessed; the Patriots were not, despite the fact that their coach at the time, Bill Parcells, was a man of God himself. As his team got stomped, Parcells might have flashed back to the 1991 Super Bowl, where, after his Giants beat the Bills, he said of the Lord, "He was playing on our side tonight." But this night the Lord switched teams (a test? punishment?) and not only answered Desmond Howard's prayers, but awarded him with the MVP trophy, which made possible his lucrative move to Oakland the following season. Thus God sanctified NFL free agency.

In sports, added edge is always sought; so it makes sense that jocks pray for game-day favors from the Most High. As Packers guard Adam Timmerman told *Sports Illustrated* in 1998, "I ask Him to keep us from injuries. And I ask for victories: 'God I want to win, so I have an even bigger platform to use for you.' People listen to winners more than they do to losers." (Pity the holy man whose team is 2–14.) Denver

Broncos running back Howard Griffith added, "It's not that we're trivializing anything. The question was posed to us: 'Does He control wins and losses?' Yes, He does." If true, does it then follow that God controls specific plays, coaching decisions, whether a runner cuts left or right? Is He consumed strictly with the NFL, or does He oversee the Canadian League? We do know He finds the NBA *fan*tastic, since so many of the league's players often call His number. Pacers guard Mark Jackson believes that "God has blessed me with a hunger and thirst to want to please Him." Mavericks forward A. C. Green credited God with helping him to regain his virginity and making chaste his life. And then there's former Knicks guard John Starks, who, after a tough playoff loss, said, "We have God on our side. His will will overcome this adversity we've been going through all year long. With Him, anything's possible." Between prayers, Starks has headbutted, trash-talked, and flagrant-fouled his way through many games. Apparently, his is the Desmond Howard brand of faith.

A few athletes are wary of their born-again teammates. "You wonder what the objective is," observed Yankees pitcher David Cone. "Is the objective the so-called spreading of the word of God, or is it to make yourself look better, or to try to conform and fit in?" When Will Clark played for the San Francisco Giants, he responded to a teammate who gave up a home run and checked it off to "God's will." "Hey, I congratulate you on doing something for your life," said Clark, himself a Catholic, "but this is about baseball. And you better get out there and do it yourself. The Lord didn't hang that slider." The season following the Minnesota Twins' World Series championship in 1987, Gary Gaetti received Christ and wished to spread the Good Word by distributing leaflets to his teammates and speaking in tongues. This did not please Kent Hrbek, who just months before was Gaetti's drinking partner. Other Twins felt similar discomfort. After three seasons as a clubhouse witness, Gaetti, fittingly enough, went to the Angels (then later to the Cardinals, then to the Cubs . . .). David Cone, Jeffersonian in outlook, once stated, "No player should be part of an environment of religious fanaticism. You ought to be able to make a choice whether you want to be a born-again Christian or not." As the number of born-agains in baseball rose, Cone was less forthcoming. He admitted it was a "hot issue" and that he held "some pretty strong sentiments about it." But, as Jefferson and indeed Lincoln before him, he was "trying to be guarded in what I'm saying."

Cone's apprehension was mild when compared to the fear felt by sports agents—reptilian creatures that bond chemically to an athlete's salary. Until recently, agents have played the percentage game almost exclusively. Those battles waged were of the traditional sort sent up in *Jerry Maguire*. But a new breed of agent now shares in the action and may, if trends continue, dominate the game itself. The Christian agent tells his client that his commission promotes the faith. And the client need never worry about the business practices of the agent, since he is saved and serves the King. One of the better-known Christian sports agencies is Champions for Christ, which operates from bases in Austin, Texas, and

Nashville, Tennessee. To adherents, CFC is less an agency than it is "an athletic ministry" devoted to "the principles of victorious Christian living." Its agents develop "strategies that deliver a Biblical message of commitment to a championship lifestyle," a sort of Pat Roberston/Tony Robbins stairway to success. To date, the majority of CFC clients are NFL players and this alarmed both team owners and non-CFC agents. The "ministry" thus came under scrutiny from the NFL and in a *Sports Illustrated* investigative piece, "Leap of Faith," by Michael Silver and Don Yaeger.

Two teams, the Chicago Bears and the Jacksonville Jaguars, asked the NFL to investigate the scope of CFC activity among their respective rosters. The Bears grew worried during contract negotiations with Penn State star running back Curtis Enis. The rookie was represented by Greg Feste, the head of a consulting firm with ties to CFC. Feste had never negotiated an NFL contract before hooking up with Enis, himself a recent convert to Christ. (Feste was once suspended for a day by the National Association of Security Dealers for dispensing bad advice to clients.) The pair put the Bears through a few ringers, including Enis's strange complaint about playing on Sundays and then his subsequent remark that he "would never play for the Bears" before he finally signed with the team for $5.6 million *over* three years—an incredibly low price for one of the top backs to come out of college. Despite their bargain, the Bears believed that Enis, as well as other Christians on the team, were being taken advantage of by CFC and its friends.* Similar beliefs surfaced

---

*A year later, Enis and Feste parted ways.

in Jacksonville, where quarterback Mark Brunell and tackle Tony Boselli gave 10 percent of their salaries to CFC. The Jaguars were also concerned with Brunell's locker room evangelism. In addition to the distribution of fliers, Brunell reportedly told teammates that they would burn in Hell unless they too joined CFC.

The NFL was limited in its options. The league couldn't force players to withhold money from agencies like CFC; and locker room disruptions caused by holy rollers were the responsibility of the team in question. In short, there was no legal way to block CFC's influence. All the league could or would do was provide team owners with information. CFC's reaction to this activity was one of bemusement and slight victimization. "All this kind of stuff, it breaks your heart," said CFC president Rice Brooks. "Here we are, going about our business quietly, ministering to athletes, preaching the Bible. People can look all they want, but really, there ain't a lot of meat on the chicken." Brooks traced the commotion to those secular agents who lost clients to CFC. "We've cost them millions of dollars," he boasted, but added that "[t]here's no money in this, believe me." (Certainly not in Enis's deal brokered by his friend Feste.) Pleased with the inroads made in the NFL, Brooks geared CFC to influence college and high school kids hungry for spiritual messages wrapped in infomercial jargon. And should Mark Brunell lead the Jaguars to Super Bowl glory, don't expect a postgame plug for Disney World (what, with *its* sodomy parades?). More likely he'll drop to his knees, wag his tongue in prayer, then stare into the nearest camera and say, "Achieve a championship lifestyle! Become a Champion for Christ today!"

The concept of marketing Christian themes in professional sports remains a radical one. Few team owners, apart from citing "God" in a safe, general way, will allow their franchises to reflect a specific denominational faith. It is thought that this will alienate segments of the paying audience, even those who tell pollsters that Jesus Christ is Lord. It seems that many fans, regardless of faith, prefer the separation of church and sport. But in Texas, where Christian enthusiasms are measured by the Richter scale, one team was packaged along Lone Star "family values" lines, while another team, reeling with sin, was reborn under God's beneficent gaze. The first team, the Texas Rangers, brought together players whose commitment to clean living and fair play were beyond question. As the Rangers' president, Tom Schieffer, told *The New York Times Magazine* during the 1997 season, "It's almost as if people are hungry for this kind of emphasis . . . People follow sports, kids in particular. If you can have people exhibiting good character and good values off the field as well as on the field, it can have a tremendously positive impact for your community."

Texas Governor George W. Bush, managing general partner and onetime owner of the Rangers, agreed. "Can a ballclub be a force for morals and values? Yes, it can—and here's why it can. People pay attention to stars—what happens on the field, and in this day and age, particularly what happens off the field. And a team can emphasize values [*sic*] . . . We know no one's perfect. But we demand decent standards of behavior from our players on the Rangers." In order to fulfill this decree, the team hired a number of decent folk like manager Johnny Oates, a favorite of the Fellowship of Christian Athletes who believed that his arrival in Texas was preordained. And then there was pitcher John Wetteland, who came south via free agency after winning the 1996 World Series with the Yankees. Wetteland, like Oates, felt a divine hand guiding his move to the Rangers, which resulted in the earthly reward of a reported $23 million. A robust witness for Christ, Wetteland, shown in *The New York Times* wearing a T-shirt that read: HOW CAN A MORAL WRONG BE A CIVIL RIGHT? (whether this referred to buggery or abortion was unclear), did not question the Lord concerning his place on the team: "You don't ask that of God. When [H]e directs you somewhere, you go."

The Rangers' strategy, bolstered by playoff appearances, paid off. Fans in and around the Arlington area, believers of varying intensity, flocked to the stadium dubbed "the Temple." And in the Rangers' clubhouse the majority of the team's players attended pregame chapel services, pondered Scripture, prayed over bats and mitts. This PR and business triumph was not lost on another team located in nearby Dallas. Despite their Super Bowl victories and Hall of Fame lineage, the Cowboys of the nineties teetered on self-destruction. Some of its players engaged in drug-taking and adultery, the most prominent of whom was All-Pro receiver Michael Irvin. At times the fun became dangerous, and a couple of Cowboys were charged with rape and assault (allegations later dropped). Even the team's coach, Barry Switzer, got into the action when he was arrested for carrying a handgun in an airport. Fueling this was an arrogance common to American success: the belief that prominence shields one from scrutiny or law, that any and all behavior is justified if practiced by celebrities. In the NFL, the Cowboys were celebrated as "America's Team." And while Cowboy boosters cheered their—our—team in sterile Texas Stadium, certain players saw the final gun as starter's pistol; once fired, they could romp like pumped-up Kennedys on spring break.

Of course, some celebrities must suffer so that other celebrities may frolic. This is certainly true in Hollywood, is becoming more so in politics, and is no different in professional sports. When the bill came due in Dallas, the Cowboys and their fans were stunned. "America's Team" made the tabloids and was hit from all sides. Owner Jerry Jones, himself no stranger to good times, had to field the charges and rumors that come with any scandal. In addition to the bad press, Dallas had a losing season and failed to make the playoffs in 1997–98 (from which, the year before, they were eliminated by the Carolina Panthers). Surely *this* was the back-breaking straw: Had the Cowboys run like the Bulls, then *perhaps* the coke and strippers found alongside Michael Irvin *could* be swept away or excused. Perhaps not. As it stood, matters seemed so out of control that Jones needed to act quickly. He convinced Switzer "to resign," as the ex-coach put it, and brought in Chan Gailey, a man anxious to meet Jesus and, if given the power, to allow prayer in public schools. Gailey was known for the inventive offensive schemes he devised for the Steelers, which, along with his religious outlook, seemed a nice mix for the "new" Cowboys. Jones then cracked down on his players and prohibited them from specific nightspots and other trouble areas. But ultimately, Jones was helped by revelation within his ranks. He had Emmitt Smith, a workhorse of Christian intensity, and he had Deion Sanders, who suddenly saw Christ on a neon cross where flashed, in bright silver and blue, new life.

The rebirth of Deion Sanders was probably his one remaining career move. Secure financially, in fine if not Prime Time physical shape, Sanders could no longer strictly play cock-of-the walk braggart who taunted and danced at the expense of opponents. The act was tired, as was Sanders himself after years of chasing tail and acquiring consumer goods. "I was never happy," he told *ESPN Magazine,* revealing his failed attempts at suicide. "I was in pain, man." Unable to find solace in material wealth and lacking a spiritual base, Sanders was typical of American celebrities in need of cosmic makeovers. Were he a kung-fu action star, he might have walked the Eastern path or perhaps had a go at Scientology. But being an athlete and accustomed to authority, Sanders chose monotheism, which in Texas means Big J Himself. After high-fiving the Lord, Sanders, energized, got busy. Instead of booty parties, he hosted Bible study classes. Instead of seducing potential sex partners, he preached the Gospel to the faithful in his church, financed with one million of his dollars. In interviews, all credit went to the Savior on Whose behalf he witnessed tirelessly. Now when he strutted on-field it was to celebrate the Lord. And lest anyone thought him insincere, Sanders did what good celebrities do once turmoil is vanquished and peace is secured: He "wrote" a book ("with" T. D. Jakes) detailing his conversion, *Power, Money, Sex—It's a Man Thing.*

Sanders has yet to complete his image makeover. There remains the spark of the con man, and it may take years of clean living and constant prayer before he is taken at his word. (Imagine Dennis Rodman as born-again: a decade-long project at best.) Athletes who cite higher powers cannot, or will not, be promoted exclusively as saints. In the commercial realm, morality works best as backdrop. Thus David Robinson, clean-cut and God-fearing, projected his goodness on to Edge shaving gel (and, by proxy, teammate Tim Duncan) and Nike clothing without mentioning the Lord. Shawn Bradley, easily the world's tallest Mormon, could have done this had he not blown off a college career in order to promote Brother Smith's vision door to door. When Bradley went pro, he became the white Manute Bol. His cameo in *Space Jam* did little to boost his commercial appeal. Companies that might have used his pure, freakish image to sell products chose instead Gheorghe Muresan, the Romanian Wizard who peddled Snickers, ESPN, and Billy Crystal, grinning dwarf to Muresan's giant.

The morality angle has worked for coaches as well. Tom Landry's firm Christian profile was exploited quite effectively in a number of amusing spots. Mike Ditka, for years semi-pyscho whenever his teams played badly, carved out a media persona that made fun of his "tense" side while showing the ex-Bear to be cuddly underneath. After a poor first season in New Orleans, Ditka predictably lost his mind but found his soul, which he surrendered to God. Now the funny, cuddly guy had religion too, a combination that could only help sell more soup or long-distance calling plans. Seahawks coach Mike Holmgren, less telegenic than Ditka, was in his modest way an effective pitchman. A partner in the NFL Coaches Outreach, a group that helps league coaches maintain "a consistent walk with Christ during the season," Holmgren used his moral weight to tell men that hair loss was not Armageddon, that dead follicles could receive new (if not everlasting) life. The savior? Rogaine. "For hair as full as His . . ."

Not all religious jocks maintain the balance necessary to lead a successful endorsement career. The spirit sends them where the secular turn to salt and are scattered by divine wind. Which brings us to Reggie White, "God's Gentle Giant" as he's been dubbed. For years White toiled in Philadelphia. A perennial All-Pro lineman, his Eagles teams never went beyond the occasional playoff appearance. No matter how bad an Eagles loss, reporters crowded around White's locker for comments and quips. Gentle Reg could be self-deprecating and funny, traits not often seen in the average NFL hulk. Over time White added Biblical proverbs to his postgame remarks, and this, according to the Christian Virtues Web site, sent reporters away from his locker. "Isn't that just like the devil," White allegedly said after a reporter bolted. "You mention the name of Jesus Christ and he just runs away." Shamed, the reporter resumed the interview. "Jesus is still Lord," insisted White. He later added, "It takes a real man to live for Jesus, not a wimp. Jesus was the greatest man who ever lived. To serve him, you have to lay down your life for him.''

To serve his rugged Savior, White lay down not just his life but his off-field career. As we've seen, companies like to have moralists promote their wares—so long as specific opinions remain private. Essence is all. White defied this rule. With the tenacity he brought upon opposing linemen and quarterbacks, White boldy extended his fundamentalist views. He was no mere player-prophet; he did not keep to arcane readings of Scripture. White dove straight into politics, economics, education, and sexuality and spoke with true candor if not full understanding of the issues. He railed against the moneychangers of pro sports and pop culture. He outlined to black youth the gap between an athlete's salary and the owner's cut of the gate. He emphasized the value of reading, told kids to learn the laws and then change them to improve their community. Of course every statement was in some way tethered to Christ, whose legend White updated. In a 1997 speech to inner-city high school students in Knoxville, Tennessee, White said that Jesus also "grew up in an inner-city area. Jesus was from the ghetto. He was from the 'hood. Go back and read it for yourself." And when it came time to administer justice, Jesus rocked with his crew. "He was the ultimate gang leader because he went out and got twelve thugs to follow him. He did! Read about it. They were hardcore fishermen.''

White seemed well-intentioned in his talks. But he tended to ramble and shoot off in odd directions. Non sequiturs flourished. In many ways, he resembled Lon Chaney,

Jr.'s character in the Bob Hope film *My Favorite Brunette:* a physically strong man-child who wants to do right but is too dim to succeed, one who is led to believe the most preposterous tales. Add to this deep superstition and an attachment to Bronze Age values and we come pretty close to Reggie White, Christian Activist. Once he became a Packer and achieved Super Bowl success, White's views on society reached a wider audience. A veteran of small venues, White was invited to speak before the Wisconsin State Assembly on March 25, 1998, and it was there he truly hit the big time. In his opening statements, he warned those assembled, "You can't get me to shut up when I get up to talk," and off he went, picking up speed every minute. He spoke of himself in the third person, a tactic all politicans understand and accept. He spoke of God, of Jesus, of healing broken homes and rebuilding communities. He spoke of his visit to the Holy Land and how this lent him perspective. "I realized something about us as Americans," he said. "We're lazy. We're extremely lazy." So far, so good. After all, he was talking about welfare cheats, right?

Perhaps. Once White takes off, it's hard to guess where he'll land. He referred to the profitable incarceration industry, where, instead of "throwing money" at social problems, Americans simply throw the poor in jail. He tried to connect the dots between class and crime, between skin color and privilege. But this proved too difficult a task. Instead, White looked to the sky for help; and God gave him the answers to the tough questions he posed. Blacks?

When you look at the black race, black people are very gifted in what we call worship and celebration. A lot of us like to dance, and if you go to black churches, you see people jumping up and down, because they really get into it.

Whites?

White people were blessed with the gift of structure and organization. You guys do a good job of building businesses and things of that nature and you know how to tap into money pretty much better than a lot of people do around the world.

Hispanics? Asians? Indians?

Hispanics are gifted in family structure. You can see a Hispanic person and they can put twenty or thirty people in one home . . . When you look at the Asians, the Asian is very gifted in creation, creativity, and inventions. If you go to Japan or any Asian country, they can turn a television into a watch . . . And you look at the Indians, they have been very gifted in the spirituality.

White babbled on. Mentioned "Touched by an Angel." Lost his place: "Where was I going with that? Where was I going? What did I say?" Found his place. Breezed through Greek and Roman history. Came to the problem that undermined those societies and now undermines ours: "As America has permitted homosexuality to establish itself as an alternate lifestyle, it is also reeling from the frightening spread of sexually transmitted disease." Explained why Jesus was seen by some as a fag: "I believe that one of the reasons that Jesus was accused of being a homosexual is because he spent time with homosexuals." Not because they were good dancers, mind you. Christ was there to heal their sickness. Homosexuals sick? Yes, said White; not only that, they're akin to liars and cheaters and backstabbers. Also, they have no rights: "I'm offended that homosexuals will say that homosexuals deserve rights." Josef Goebbels was equally offended, but White didn't cover that part of history.

Well, to be fair, he skated past it. "In the process of history, homosexuals have never been castrated [never?], millions of them never died." Certainly thousands were rounded up and put in death camps, some shot, some left to waste. But not "millions," so they really have nothing to cry about. After all, "Homosexuality is a decision. It's not a race." As he denounced all things queer, White praised the achievements of the Greek heterosexuals Socrates, Plato, and Aristotle, "a dazzling roster of men" who oversaw "democracy, splendid architecture, [and] excellence in culture." He seemed impressed with the Roman Empire's strength and military conquests, perhaps unaware of the sexual tendencies of Rome's various Caesars and the rather "open" policy of its legions. No matter. Rome was doomed once it took seriously Greek philosophy "with its humanistic and garish base" (so much for its "excellence"), committed itself to "big government," and let the homos freely cruise. Rome lacked what America lacks, discipline, something the White home abounds in. "I don't need to hit my kids more than five times when I whoop them, because I don't want to go and get angry at them," confessed White. "But those five licks they still remember from two years ago, and I have two of the best kids in the world and two of the most honest kids in the world."

The connection between "discipline" and a latent fear of fags is an interesting one. The need to remain "straight" at all times consumes the conscious mind as it warps unconscious thought. What struggles must go on from tailgate party to locker room shower! No other fan and player base is more queer-phobic than football's, and Reggie White's beliefs, while based in Scripture, are no different than that of any group of guys in the cheap seats, drinking beer. There is nothing more frightening to men who like to watch bigger men grab and bang each other than the prospect of faggot jocks. If there are players in the NFL who prefer cock to pussy, the gladiator myth crashes to artificial turf and all hell breaks loose.* Thus any suggestion that the NFL is less than 100 percent heterosexual is laughed away, dismissed. Fags are sissies who wear women's clothes. Real men don shoulder pads and extremely tight pants that highlight the contours of their asses and units—especially when they bend over in a three-point stance where quarterbacks and running backs can get a good look at both.

---

*Conversely, the myth that all women athletes prefer pussy to cock was played down by the WNBA, especially when it became clear that the league had a loyal dyke following. Players with kids were spotlighted to promote the league's "wholesome" image and make it a fun place for girls to see their role models—who must be and are as straight as a baseline.

In the history of pro football, only three men are known for their same-sex desires: Dave Kopay, a journeyman running back and special teams player known for his drive and intensity; Jerry Smith, an All-Pro tight end for the Redskins who died of AIDS in 1986; and Roy Simmons, a guard for the Giants who in 1992 came out, then quietly went away. Of the trio it was Kopay who garnered, and occasionally garners, media attention. His autobiography was published in 1977 at the dawn of what now is called "the religious right," then personified by Anita Bryant who feared a fag takeover of America that would mean no more breeding, so "there would be no sports, no spectators, and no human life." Luckily the boys were too busy partying and creating new diseases fatal to them instead of her—and us, happy spectators spared God's wrath. Yet Kopay was spared too. His book, *The Dave Kopay Story: An Extraordinary Self-Revelation* (with Perry Deane Young), opened that door so long kept sealed by gentlemen's agreement: the sexual proclivities of NFL players.

Amazingly, there were, and doubtless are, a fair number of queers who suited up each Sunday to do battle. Kopay had sex with some of them, though he has never named names and refuses to speculate on contemporary players, a position he honors to the present day. He simply made the obvious point that football is no different from other areas of life. Where there are people there are different tastes in music, clothes, and sex; the like-minded usually find one another and share enthusiasms, preferences. The NFL is unique only in that this is done between men who are physically large and strong and conditioned to wreak havoc on weekends.

Kopay's book is a chronicle of his journey down this road where he wore the uniforms of the 49ers, Lions, Redskins, Saints, and Packers (pre-Reggie) and played for "Mr. Winning Is the Only Thing," Vince Lombardi, when the legend coached in Washington before succumbing to cancer. At some point during his journey, a manipulated prostate served as Kopay's alarm bell. After several attempts to suppress his nature (marriage, hypnosis), Kopay accepted matters, eventually retired, and came out. His book was a bestseller, which meant media exposure and a brief public glance into the NFL's walk-in closet. Then, salacious appetite sated (save for the supermarket rags), media attention dwindled. Over the years, Kopay was intermittently sought by journalists who asked the same questions that others asked before them. Kopay repeated the obvious, reacted to new insults, the Reggie White speech being one. He was invited to respond to White by *The New York Times,* the same paper that many years earlier spiked a favorable review of *The Dave Kopay Story* written by Dave Anderson. Apparently the *Times* had lightened up,* unlike the NFL. White received a few tsk-tsks from league sources, but then how offended could they get, since the NFL is homosexual-free?

The worst hits Reggie White took were, of course, com-

---

*At least when it came to Kopay and White. In a special Sunday *Magazine* issue devoted to women's basketball ("A Sport You Can Love," August 16, 1998), the *Times* avoided any mention of dykes in and around the WNBA and the now-defunct ABL. It was, instead, a promo sheet worthy of anything put out by the NFL. "Lesbian chic" did not extend to female jocks and their fans.

mercial ones. He considered retirement and was negotiating with CBS to announce and analyze games when the text of his speech was made public. The Tiffany Network backed away, as did other sponsors, including Chunky Soup, which White had endorsed with the rather tantalizing line, "It's loaded with beef!" Nike chairman Phil Knight added his thoughts, saying that White was "in the simplest terms not evil, he's just crazy." But then in one of his more lucid moments, White had denounced the slave-labor conditions in Nike's plants overseas. This is what most likely peeved Knight, though he might also have seen White as a PR buffoon, hence "crazy." (As for evil, see Chapter 4.) White responded that he was indifferent to his critics. All that mattered was his relationship to God, Who told White to forgo retirement and to play one more season with the Packers. Fallout from the speech remained, but some in the public eye, like Christian presidential candidate Gary Bauer and Confederacy buff Senator Trent Lott, embraced White and his views. The NFL continued to practice "don't ask, don't tell" while fans remained lost in gladiator reverie, melted cheese dripping from their chapped, parted lips.

Of course, the NFL is not alone in its denial. Every major league, every college and high school athletic department does the same, for the alternative is far too dangerous and upsetting. So until the day when Notre Dame's Touchdown Jesus comes to life and renders Judgment on this and other evils (exclusive broadcast rights owned by Fox Sports), the beat, as it were, will go on.

2
Blood & Guts

Serious sport has nothing to do with fair play. It is bound up with hatred, jealousy, boastfulness, disregard for all rules, and sadistic pleasure in witnessing violence: in other words, it is war minus the shooting.

——GEORGE ORWELL

Hey, baby, this movie is rated R. Adult language and violence. Lots of it.

——BRUCE SMITH, BUFFALO BILLS

Whenever a black athlete celebrates a score, the little Klansman inside most American white men stands and clenches his jaw. Every hip-shaking, head-tossing, fist-pumping display sends even "civilized" Caucasians into redneck fits of disgust. An uncomfortable truth but quite so. In fact, this happens more to white-collar types than to actual rednecks for the simple reason that the latter openly shows his hates and fears. Since nothing is repressed, there is no need for release, at least not the kind that doubles up those who hold it all in.

Also, as Jim Goad explained in *The Redneck Manifesto,* crackers have more in common with the descendants of Ham than they do with their elite brethren—another uncomfortable, but inescapable, truth. Given their cultural affinities with blacks, rednecks may share some of the elation shown in end zone dances. After all, they too jump and grind with a black grace of their own, movements unknown to white boys farther up society's ladder. But despite this (genetic?) advantage, rednecks will usually side with their economic betters once a black receiver breaks loose at midfield, sprints down the sidelines to the ten, where, after a quick glance over his shoulder, the flaunting begins: shimmy and shakes; head rolling as if free of neck; knees brought up in swift, chorus line jerks. Touchdown. The helmet comes off, the receiver yells he's the shit, and the executive and carpenter watching feel a twist in their stomachs as the little Klansman ties a noose and waits for sundown.

The sports sociologist Harry Edwards has described end zone celebrations as extensions of black creativity, improv sessions that recall the heydey of Birdland. There is a theatrical, musical element to these displays which cannot be denied, but as a creative form the end zone dance ranks alongside the victory struts of professional wrestlers. And since it is a form easily learned, we now see it all over the field through most of the game. Whether a punt returner is nailed where he catches the ball, a pass is knocked away from a receiver's hands, or a quarterback is thrown for a loss, those in on the play whoop it up, bump chests, clang helmets, and, yes, dance. The common is made spectacular through the unchanneled flow of testosterone, which may explain why the true fans of this behavior are adolescent boys and teens whose balls are as juiced as the athletes they admire. Testosterone is color-blind, but to some observers the ritual of celebration stems primarily from da niggaz. "It's the showmanship, it's in your face, it's fuck you . . . it's all of that," author Nelson George has said. "It's a black male thing that comes right out of the street, schoolyard ball, intimidation. It comes from the same root."

If blacks are indeed revved by fuck-you showmanship, what then of whites who get damp from the same source? What motivates them? Science offers few answers. Sociologists pose questions of such length that it takes hours for the answers to arrive, by which point new questions emerge, the answers even longer in coming. (An endless cycle, this.) Sports analysts add nothing, consumed as they are with personalities and stats. So long as the rubes don't litter the field with bottles and garbage, their motivations are of no real interest. For this one must trust instinct and the evidence of one's eyes. And after watching televised games with alternating sets of white men in different surroundings (snowed-in taverns, Gulf Coast huts, interstate weigh stations with satellite hookups), this observer believes that many white men, inner-Nazis aside, are transfixed by black flesh in motion. Dizziness occurs. The decline of oxygen in their brains causes hoots and yells consistent with mammals in heat. Whites succumb to primal urges and go full monkey mad. Perhaps this is why, equilibrium returned, they despise black jocks in celebration. They feel used, vulnerable. Their enjoyment rouses deeper fears, which they try desperately to avoid but cannot. The fear is in their face, taunting them, shaking its head, pounding its chest.

Whatever logic underlies the twisted white love of black athletes, we'll never approach it. Collective denial is too strong, too deep. Instead, we are shown panel discussions that deal with surface issues; fantasylands, where all share the same point of reference. Differences arise, but these are well-meaning diversions from the topic at hand. A sterling example of this was President Clinton's Town Hall meeting on race and sports held in Houston on April 14, 1998. It was typical of Clinton's other "town meetings" on race: Real antagonisms were kept from view while a "civil" discourse prevailed. One half-expected Disney mascots to rush the stage and rub the heads of the panelists. Jim Brown alone spoke of broader issues and asked unsettling questions. The NFL great wanted answers regarding wealthy black athletes and their connection to their respective communities. His hits on Nike pawns Michael Jordan and Tiger Woods drew defensive retorts from company loyalists Jackie-Joyner Kersee and John Thompson, who said that to him education is a matter of market positioning. But the opportunity to expand on these issues passed as Clinton moved on to less pressing, more uplifting topics.

When one considers race and sports, a better conversation comes to mind. After all, if the point is to highlight the problems of race hatred in the context of national pastimes, then racists and hustlers should be included. Where was Marge Schott? Bobby Hull? Don King? Even Khalid Abdul-Muhammad would have a few pointed comments regarding the issue. A roundtable featuring these personalities would generate big ratings, and the collision of biases might yield a stimulating exchange—perhaps *too* stimulating for most Americans to endure. While Schott and Abdul-Muhammad would undoubtedly clash over black vs. white (with Don

King smiling and shouting, "Yes, sir!"), they, along with Bobby Hull, might agree that while one man's cracker is another man's nigger, no one is more devious than the Jews. A TECHNICAL DIFFICULTIES graphic flashes on; the studio is cleared; the roundtable is replaced with a Classic Sports telecast of Game 6 of the 1978 NBA Finals between the Bullets and the Sonics.

In America, racism should not exist and so, save for the occasional black man dragged to his death in Texas, does not. American sports are especially clean of this contagion. Just ask George Will. The mere utterance of the word *racism* will inspire in him a withering look, rodentian eyes dilating behind wire frames. Why, how can racism exist when Michael Jordan makes so much money! And he's popular to boot! Look at all those white kids who want his autograph! Using celebrity culture to downplay or deny societal ills is a popular tactic among many writers and columnists, and it resonates. By cheering for Jordan or buying books recommended by Oprah, whites are somehow absolved of their hatred for single black mothers in the projects.

The denial of race hatred extends to team symbols. For years many native American groups have protested the use of Indian caricatures on caps and helmets, as well as certain rituals practiced by fans. One such ritual, the Tomahawk Chop, raised the hackles of those whose ancestors were slaughtered by European settlers (assuming, of course, that a rival tribe didn't murder them first). Developed by Florida State boosters, whose football Seminoles are a perennial Top 5 team which naturally drives them to frenzy, the Chop was adopted by Atlanta Braves fans. There, under Ted Turner's gaze, the ritual went national, highlighted by an ongoing Braves presence in the playoffs and occasional World Series. The Chop was done two ways: 1) the hand flat as a blade brought down in a robotic chopping motion; and 2) through the use of a foam tomahawk brought down in similar fashion. Whenever the Braves rallied, their fans would begin chopping while bellowing an odd tribal chant. It sounded like something from an old Hollywood film where Jeff Chandler or Victor Mature played Indian warriors. Whatever the source, Braves fans loved the Chop. It provided comfort and gave them hope during innings when all seemed lost. Even Mrs. Turner, Jane Fonda, submitted to its power and did her liberal guilt version of the Chop—a quick downward slash—trusting that no real Indian saw her.

Well, a good number did. And to no one's surprise they were appalled. Not by Fonda per se, whose connection to native tradition consisted of breeding buffaloes for their meat. Indian activists were sickened by the entire spectacle and deemed the Chop a cultural affront. Protests were lodged; small demonstrations staged. But in the end nobody cared what they or any other savage thought. The Chop was an intrinsic part of the Braves experience. Fans had a First Amendment right to wave their arms and emit war chants. It was fun for the kids. Whatever the excuse, it was clear that Braves fans were not going to give up their ritual. And when the Braves faced the Cleveland Indians in the 1995 World Series, the excuses grew louder and shriller. A din was created by fans, players, and sportswriters sympathetic to both teams in order to drown out the inevitable complaints. For not only did this Series have the Chop, it had the grinning Indian face on the caps of Cleveland's players, Chief Wahoo. The Braves were bad enough; but this image *truly* sent activists spinning. As a caricature, the Chief is a Red Sambo—big teeth, wide eyes, hooked nose. Were it representative of any other ethnic group, especially one with political clout, the smilin' Injun would be history. Instead, it is worn as a badge of defiance and honor.

Those defiant claim to rebel against an all-powerful force known as "political correctness." The PC Nazis desire nothing less than the complete elimination of every Indian reference in sports. They've scored several victories: the St. John's Redmen were changed to the Red Storm; the Stanford Indians became the Cardinal (singular noun: a very large bird indeed). A number of high schools met with similar fates. But the pros have proven resilient. Even the Washington Redskins, an anti-Indian slur equivalent to coon, yid, spic, and gook, remain unaffected by the PC onslaught—for now . . .

Those who resist this assault on tradition employ several methods of defense. One is to point to other team symbols like Notre Dame's Fighting Irish and Minnesota's Vikings and say, "Nobody complains about *them*." This diversionary tactic usually works but is logically deficient. Notre Dame's aggressive leprechaun is not forced upon those of Irish descent. It is embraced. If it wasn't, it would be gone. As for Norse descendents who feel connected to Viking lore, what would be their complaint? The rituals that some Minnesota boosters act out in the stands play off the mythology of Thor (at least the one celebrated in Marvel Comics) with a touch of Valkyrie chic. Kitsch to be sure, but not the kind that prances and hoots atop mass graves.

This brings us to another traditionalist defense strategy, that Indian symbols are a collective homage to a once-proud people. It is a claim often made in straight, solemn tones, as though the ghosts of native warriors linger nearby. One may immediately dismiss such claims as spurious, primarily in the case of the Redskins (in what way is *that* a tribute?). The concept of honoring said traditions, taken simply at its face, suggests that native cultures were always so honored, which of course is false. It was only after the red man fell before the white that the conquerer felt some respect for the vanquished. Let's use the ever-handy Nazi parallel. Say the Third Reich survived World War II, its camps and ovens intact, and decreed that enough Jews and Gypsies had been exterminated. No longer seen as a threat to the Nazi state, survivors were set up in various communities and allowed to practice their customs in private. Over time, Germans felt some guilt for what had been done and respected those victims who put up a fight. To honor their memory, German soccer teams adopted several names: the Berlin Kikes, the Hamburg Gyps, the Munich Hebrews, and the Bremen Rabbis, whose mascot was a dancing Orthodox Jew who led Rabbi fans in Hebraic chants as they waved rams horns and tossed yarmulkes onto the field after scores. When asked the meaning of the ritual, a Rabbis fan, face painted in Star of David blue, replies, "It's a tribute to *das Juden*. Besides, *das kinder* love it!"

The Cleveland Indians symbol is no different from any hook-nosed Jewish caricature, yet it is seen by Cleveland fans as the acme of pride and tradition. Were those who defend this symbol truly interested in tradition, they would demand a full-scale homage to Louis Sockalexis, a Penobscot Indian from Maine who was the first Native American* to play pro baseball. He came to Cleveland in 1897 when the town's club was called the Spiders. Sockalexis batted .338 that year, and during his three seasons with the club he averaged .313. In the years following Sockalexis's departure the Spiders became the Blues, the Bronchos, and then the Naps. In 1915, in response to a contest to rename the team, a local fan suggested the Indians in honor of Sockalexis. This was of course done, but as time passed, the man who inspired the Indian name vanished as Chief Wahoo came into view. Like the Redskins, whose symbol is quite noble despite the team name, the Indians and their fans honor nothing save the Hollywood western and theatrical cartoons of the 1940s. How interesting and radical it would be were the Indians to use Sockalexis as its symbol. A likeness of his stoic features, say in the style of R. Crumb's blues portraits, would be infinitely better than the current model. The Indian moniker would then be linked to something—someone—tangible. If the Cubs can wear a drawing of their late announcer Harry Caray on their uniform sleeves, what's Cleveland's excuse?

Race hatred works best when it is unspoken. In sports this is the preferred method. After all, team owners cannot win

*Used for lack of a more precise term. "Migratory Siberians," while nice, suggests restlessness, flight.

71

without colored folk, hence the delightful images of rich white guys mixing with the lower breeds, slapping backs, exchanging hugs. This requires keen acting skills on the part of owners and their front office minions since few of them spend their off-hours hanging with Leroy or Enriqué. The scenery occasionally shifts. Football and basketball have slowly, slowly integrated their respective executive ranks, though neither would startle the average Texaco VP. Baseball, however, remains as pale as hockey. Whites rule. Masterfully played down, baseball's racist impulse surges at certain times to remind us of who runs the show and for whom the show is staged.

The Mark McGwire/Sammy Sosa home run race was such a reminder. Having come near the magic 61 home run mark in 1997, McGwire was expected to break Roger Maris's record the following year—not only expected but officially cheered on. Baseball, it was felt, needed a larger-than-life hero to stem fan defections from the game (caused by the '94 strike) and to attract a newer, younger audience accustomed to faster, flashier pastimes. Fans, we were told, wanted shows of power, not pitching duels or stolen bases or strategies in the field. Gold Gloves were nice but in the grand scheme unimportant. Baseball had to go Nintendo, and McGwire was the perfect character to lead fans through the home run odyssey maze. More, he played up the hype. "I can overcome almost anything I want to overcome with the strength of my mind," he told the press, conjuring images of a brain with bulging hemispheres. As the 1998 season progressed, it was clear that the Cardinals were going nowhere. No matter. Fans filled Busch Stadium to see baseball's official mascot whack 'em out.

McGwire stayed ahead of his nearest competitor and co-mascot, Ken Griffey, Jr., whose stroke was as sweet as McGwire's was blunt. But Griffey suffered homer slumps (of the kind average players would kill for) and in the final third of the season was surpassed by the Cubs' right fielder Sammy Sosa.

Sosa's run on McGwire caught many by surprise. He wasn't an official mascot; he barely spoke English. His appearance on the home run stage seemed a joke, like his name. Yet Sosa kept pace with McGwire; and once it became obvious that he was in the race to stay, his character had to be defined. Since Big Mac was the All-American boy, raised in Southern California, a graduate of USC, Sosa the Dominican was made his comic sidekick: less Sancho Panza (McGwire was no wayward Quixote), more a smiling Tonto to McGwire's Lone Ranger, Sammy the Black Cub to Mark Bunyan. Though everyone conceded that Sosa would also break 61, baseball's elite had annointed McGwire as Maris's successor, so as the record came into sight, the hype accelerated on his behalf. Culmination came September 8 when McGwire hit number 62, a line drive that just cleared the left-field fence. That it came during a two-game homestand against Chicago provided added punch. Sosa was there to show his support and to jump into McGwire's arms while the Maris family looked on and applauded. The late Yankee's offspring were strategically placed a few rows behind the Cardinal dugout so McGwire could reach them quickly, share hugs, say that Roger was with him when the winner was hit.

The spectacle was typically American: staged emotion (something McGwire's genuine glee could not overcome), endless ovations, near-religious wailing. It was an official coronation with commissioner Bud Selig there to set the crown on McGwire's head. Fox Sports televised the proceedings and played to every cliché imaginable, including the line that McGwire's feat was not only great for baseball, but a boost for the country at large. Fox, in tandem with ESPN, had helped build the hype by breaking into other games to show McGwire's at-bats, and this exclusive focus reeled in casual observers taken with the spectacle. The nonsports media helped too, informing their consumers that Big Mac's chase was Important. Everyone, it seemed, had to be happy because this was a Good Thing. When McGwire finally broke the record, APPLAUSE signs flashed with strobe-light intensity, commentators spoke as though the savior arrived, fans wiped tears from each other's cheeks. After the game, in full view of the press, Selig awarded McGwire with something called the Personal Achievement Award. McGwire flexed his huge arms and said that he was "like in awe of myself." Totally.

And what of Sammy Sosa? Well, he knew his place and so had the label CLASS ACT slapped on his forehead by appreciative sports anchors. After all, he more or less crashed McGwire's rolling party of fun, so it was best that he remained in the background. But while Sosa was humble, his bat was plain fucking rude; and the height of this rudeness was seen on Wrigley Field, September 13, where against the Brewers Sosa hit numbers 61 and 62. Cubs fans were ecstatic, as were Sosa's teammates. Yet the celebration was modest in tone compared to the McGwire blast. No one from the Maris family was present; nor was Bud Selig; nor was Fox Sports, which earlier that week practically humped McGwire with its cameras. ESPN cut into its golf broadcast with live Sosa at-bats. Only the Dominican Republic bothered to carry the Cubs/Brewers game in its entirety, after which Sosa received congratulatory (and presumably noncollect) calls from Randy Maris and Selig, who, ninety miles away in Milwaukee, found the time to grab a phone. That Sosa broke Ruth's *and* Maris's record in the same game to tie McGwire evidently meant little to the baseball elite. Their indifference to Sosa's achievement was breathtaking, to say the least.

Criticism was heard from various corners, including a fine, nasty piece by Wallace Matthews in *The New York Post.* Some believed that a racist double standard was in effect, but this was quickly denied by followers of "The Mark Show." Oprah, MJ, and Cosby were hauled out once again to disprove the ridiculous notion that race matters in contemporary America. Some, like *Washington Post* columnist Charles Krauthammer, added Ken Griffey, Jr., to the list of popular Negroes and said that had the Mariners' slugger matched McGwire, white fans would have been equally thrilled. Sosa was simply not on either player's hitting level, his remarkable performance aside. Like the Orioles' Brady Anderson, who in 1996 hit 50 homers, Sosa was a one-season wonder. He lacked the Ruthian splendor of McGwire, for whom home runs were genetically coded. McGwire earned his acclaim through superior talent. Sosa, by comparison, was a fluke.* However skin color did nothing to shape this

*Krauthammer's observation was proven ridiculous by Sosa's strong performance the following season.

perception. Sosa himself said, "Mark is the man" when he acknowledged the big guy's dominance. What further proof did one need?

It was true that many whites pulled for Sosa—they were primarily Cubs fans, but others spoke fondly of Sammy and his quest. (There were those white centrists who hoped for a tie.) A large chunk of the Spanish-speaking populace, especially Dominicans, rooted for Sosa on strictly nationalist grounds. For every proud Dominican shown soaping Sosa's name and number of homers on his car windshield, there was a proud white native telling reporters that "Americans made the record, and Americans should break the record." Black natives also backed McGwire "because he's an American," as one Atlanta man said to *The New York Times*. "Sosa's a brother, and I'm a brother. But McGwire's an American." It appeared that fans were divided more along borderlines than along color lines, and this provided columnists like Krauthammer the ammunition they needed to shoot down the race angle. But those who criticized the manner in which the home run derby was framed centered their complaints on baseball's owners, not the fans. It was, after all, their show, and they ran it in predictably crude fashion. Race may have been a nonissue for many fans, but it clearly mattered to baseball's elite. It is inconceivable that a white player who hit as many homers as Sosa would have been treated as shabbily as was he.

Sosa's stoicism was remarkable, given that he was smacked in the face by the very people who praised his humility. No doubt money played its standard role. After all, Sosa grew up poor and was now making millions. Had he uttered a peep in his defense, he would have been reminded of this fact and told that he was ungrateful. Better to enjoy the ride and take personal satisfaction in his achievement. As Sosa told the media at season's end, before anyone can approach McGwire's final tally of 70 home runs, they must first beat his 66—a daunting task in itself.* After a brief (and unproductive) playoff appearance and a PR tour of Japan, Sosa finally surpassed McGwire when he was voted the National League's Most Valuable Player by the Baseball Writers' Association. It was belated but deserved recognition of Sosa's accomplishments that helped to erase, but did not mitigate, his mistreatment at the hands of the McGwire faithful. In fact, some of those who felt that Big Mac reinvented baseball that year were mortified by the decision. "McGwire just can't catch a break," sighed Alan Schwarz in *The New York Times.* Schwarz conceded that Sosa was indeed valuable to his playoff-bound Cubs, but that McGwire was valuable "to the popularity of the sport itself," as though the MVP award should honor a player's contribution to league marketing as well as, or perhaps instead of, to his team. No serious person would say that McGwire was overlooked or slighted in 1998; yet when he lost to Sosa in the balloting (and finished sixth or seventh on several ballots) McGwire defenders like Schwarz made this very claim.†

*On the other hand when one considers the smaller parks, the juiced balls and the mediocre pitching, it may not be long before a 66-home-run season is as common as a 30-home-run season is now.

†Good thing that Josh Gibson's 84 homers hit during the 1936 season were never seriously considered or who knows how much wailing we might have heard. Happily, Gibson's feat is seen as irrelevant because Gibson played in the Negro League which, as everyone knows, was inferior to the dominant white leagues . . . except in those exhibition games where the white boys were beaten like farm hands caught in the dark part of town.

McGwire's homerama supposedly brought new fans to the old pastime. Certainly those who clogged outfield walkways in pursuit of a Big Mac special wouldn't have been there unless history was being made. And once McGwire reached 60 the dream of many was to catch the tying and record-breaking homers and then cash in the balls. What could be more American? But baseball showed its true color yet again when it announced that the IRS would pocket most of whatever one could get for a McGwire-hit ball. As the sportswriter Wallace Matthews put it, "[A]m I the only one offended that baseball—having cashed in on the fans, big time, for years selling overpriced memorabilia—now threatens to have [the] IRS 'Al Capone' any fan who tries to share in the gravy train?" And instead of taking their chances and calling the major league's bluff, those who did catch McGwire's subsequent home run balls obediently returned them in exchange for handshakes, autographed jerseys, photos with the star. To again cite Matthews, "baseball has been dumbed-down and pumped-up in an effort to attract the masses." Judging from fan conduct it appeared that the effort was a success. The masses, true to form, allowed themselves to be led by the nose until they slammed into an outfield wall.*

As crass as baseball was that mercenary season, the behavior of fans who chased McGwire's and Sosa's home run balls was equally bad. Like Russians fighting for bread, mobs of prospective ball merchants punched, kicked, bit, gouged,

*McGwire's 70th home run ball was eventually sold at auction for $3 million to Todd MacFarlane, creator of *Spawn*. From the bat of one millionaire into the collection of another: Thus does nature work.

and beat down anyone who held the red-stitched prize. Age, size, even physical infirmity did nothing to deter those crazed by the hunt. If you somehow came up with the genuine article, there were a dozen thugs ready to split your skull and take your arm. The action outside Wrigley Field was especially frightening to watch. When Sosa hit number 61 out of the park and into the street, a mob knocked over a wheelchair-bound man as it chased the ball, indifferent to his condition. Later, when number 62 also hit the street outside Wrigley, the poor bastard who grabbed the ball was slammed to the pavement by two thugs, one of whom bit into the hand clutching the treasure. While the actions of these Cubs fans (one assumes they were such) may seem extreme, it was the inevitable reaction to the hype surrounding the home run race, and the logical extension of the cruelty dispensed by those "into" their team.

Stick with Cubs fans for a moment. For years the infamous Bleacher Bums of Wrigley were known to toss batteries and live mice at opposing right fielders. And then there is the mandatory practice of throwing the enemy team's home run balls back onto the field, Chicago's version of "Fuck you, pal." But for sheer fun nothing beats shouting racial epithets at rival outfielders. This is commonly accepted by black players visiting Wrigley, and the torrent of slurs seems strongest in the right-field bleachers. Ex-Met Butch Huskey experienced this early in the 1998 season after he smacked a second-inning homer off Cubs starter Jeremi Gonzalez. When Huskey returned to his postion in right field at the bottom of the inning, the Bums let him have it. He absorbed a steady amount of abuse before he turned to the crowd and imitated Sammy Sosa's gesture, two fingers on the heart followed by a blown kiss. "I thought maybe if I did that, they would laugh and say, 'OK, maybe he's a good guy.' But it added gasoline to the fire," said Huskey. Former Cub Brian McRae added that the Bums are as organic to Wrigley as the ivy. "What can we do except shut 'em up by winning ballgames?"

Of course, race alone does not fuel such fan behavior. A hearty mix of resentment, frustration, fantasy, desire, primate urges, and tribal passion does the trick. Little appeases this type of beast save for countless victories and championships, and even then the animal remains on edge. Why? Some believe that environment determines the change; that a decent individual, after prolonged bleacher exposure, will say and do things that he finds repulsive in his private life. Others point to breeding, genetic makeup, and bell curves. Still others say a combination of elements come into play, that any fan can become a drooling, mindless lunatic, but it takes a determined effort to reach that state where objective reality turns into subjective partisan madness.

In Yankee Stadium's right-field bleachers, the effort is openly and successfully made. As in Chicago, these Yankees fans operate under a collective title, Bleacher Creatures. Here the monosyllable reigns supreme. Home team devotion is expressed in grunts and chants as a cowbell clangs and beer cups are popped by a booze hound's foot. High-fives are done in triplicate; logos representing enemy teams, whether on

shirt or cap, are aggressively suppressed.* And while there
are similar types of behavior in other parts of the Stadium
(including spitting and pouring beer on people's heads,
throwing batteries and bottles at the opposing team's bull-
pen), the Creatures perform their rites with a certain theatrical edge. It's been rumored that their allegiance is
literally fed with the internal organs of Yankee legends
tossed their way like meat in a cage. The Creatures apparently believe that consumption of the organs will lead
them to a place of spirits where reside the Yankee greats—
Mickey Mantle's liver as peyote button. When they return
from this pinstriped astral state, they feel bonded to the
team for life and wait for the next legend to drop. When
DiMaggio died, many lined up to take the ultimate trip.
But Joltin' Joe was whisked to San Francisco, and the Creatures, denied, made do with beer and thoughts of Berra,
Rizzuto, and Catfish Hunter.

Some Yankees fans are prone to violence as well. They
usually assault one another, section stalking section, class
warfare between box and bleacher seats. But heaven help
those who foolishly don opposing colors and stroll in the
direction of drunk Yankees boosters. This simply is unwise.
And it doesn't matter if the opposing fan is on his own turf:
Yankees fans respect no boundaries, so consumed are they

---

*If possible, the enemy team itself is undermined. Recall young Jeffrey
Maier, who in Game 1 of the 1996 ALCS reached over the right-field fence
and grabbed a Derek Jeter fly ball that was about to be caught by the
Orioles' Tony Tarasco. Instead of receiving a ground rule double due to
fan interference, Jeter was awarded a home run, which helped the Yankees
win a tight game. Maier was feted by delirious New Yorkers, Mayor Giuli-
ani included, who taught the boy that no rule applies so long as victory is
secured. Another Creature was made.

with their team's place in the cosmos. During a 1998 inter-league game with the Mets at Shea Stadium, two Yankees fans attacked a Mets fan near a concession stand. The victim's jaw was broken and his teeth knocked through his lip. To be expected. After all, this was the best season the Bombers had experienced in decades; how could someone root *against* them—in New York no less?! (The assailants reportedly got probation based on this defense, plus 10 percent off all beer purchases at the following Yankees home game.)

But Yankees fans are not unique in their need to physically express themselves. Their rivals in the American League East, the Boston Red Sox, have a rich history of fan dementia. In the century's early years, when the Yanks were mere Highlanders, Sox rooters would march on the field before games, waving banners, singing Irish songs. Not even the cops dared confront them, except in extreme cases. As years passed and the great Sox players of the 1910s and early '20s were sold off (the most celebrated of whom was Babe Ruth), Fenway Park became the Field of Anguish. For every Ted Williams and Carl Yastremzski there was Tony Conigliaro, his face disfigured by a fastball, and Bill Buckner, whose infamous error in the 1986 World Series led to a Mets victory and his ultimate disgrace in Beantown. Buckner was never forgiven by Sox fans for allowing Mookie Wilson's grounder to roll between his legs. He and his family were run out of Boston like pork-eaters driven from Kabul. Buckner's exile serves as a warning to those who wear the Red Sox uniform. And if the fans had their way, Buckner's head would have been impaled on the right-field foul pole, Mookie's Topps card stuck in its mouth.*

If baseball, an idyllic game where the scent of warm peanuts blends with that of freshly cut grass, can inspire this kind of mania, what then of football, the aggressor's pastime? Truly, nothing says AMERICA like NFL Sunday. That drunken sense of Manifest Destiny, that vicarious surge of brute energy, the screams, the shouts, the eyes-rolled-back view of absolute triumph—this defines the real NFL fan. Amid stadium debris and living room clutter, the overfed beast roams, his mind packed with helmet-cam shots, his ears acute as sideline mikes. To him the collision of padded meat is a crescendo so sublime it must be felt rather than heard; a vibe that rattles his breastplate, thickens his blood, fractures his mind. But if experienced for too long, the ride becomes dangerous. Few beasts negotiate these feelings through four quarters without a breakdown of some kind. It is comparable to filling a baboon with mescal, then sending him whitewater kayaking, minus paddle and helmet, as rocks fall randomly around him. The rush of events and the strain to stay balanced will so violently bend his mind that should he survive the rapids he'll either collapse in a wet heap and fetally regress, or he'll tear out the throats of everyone within reach and fashion them as pennants.

Where do NFL fans show the heartiest devotion? A random search of league cities does establish a crude pecking

---

*Let us not forget those Phillies fanatics who threatened the lives of Mitch Williams's children when he lost Game 6 of the 1993 World Series to the Toronto Blue Jays. Williams, a hard-throwing closer, was forced to leave the City of Brotherly Love in order to protect his family.

order, though this does not mean that some teams are bereft of crazed followers. Where there is football, there are maniacs. But certain patterns do emerge. For instance, teams that play in domed stadiums have fewer people who paint their upper torsos and drink until they vomit on the railings. Climate control explains part of this; after all, the whole point of painting one's body in team colors is to display one's allegiance despite weather conditions. Domes render this moot. One might think that a constant temperature of, say, 68 degrees would inspire the dedicated fan to transcend his artificial environment through extremist measures (scarification with broken beer bottles, self-immolation using everclear). Instead, the reverse usually happens: The fan settles into a comfort zone, leans this way and that with the crowd, rises when the action on-field heats up. In place of sun and clouds, the intricate latticework of the dome's ceiling, which has a soothing narcotic effect on those who stare up at it. In place of grass, bright artificial turf, a pretty carpet that invokes the familiar warmth of the Brady's backyard. All else is concrete and metal. From Seattle to New Orleans, the same story every Sunday: anthropoidal violence as an indoor leisure service. No need to go nuts.

Domed stadiums also pacify those on the sidelines. Consider Mike Ditka. Outdoors on Chicago's Soldier Field, he terrorized his players at the slightest infraction. Under the Louisiana Superdome, Ditka was broken within two seasons. Instead of blind anger, he waved Galilean palm fronds in reaction to a Saints fumble or interception. One wonders if Bud Grant would have succumbed as easily as Ditka. When

Grant coached the Vikings, they played in the cold of Metro-
politan Stadium. Heaters were banned from the team's sideline; players had to endure the frigid Minnesota temperatures
with the same silent grit as their coach. Although he led the
Vikings to three Super Bowls, Grant never won a ring.

After Grant's retirement, his winter-resistant team moved
into the Metrodome. Now when the Vikings play in the cold
of Green Bay or Chicago, they are seen as disadvantaged because they are a "dome" team—a fate Grant could not have
foreseen or perhaps wished not to foresee.* If there is a
heaven for Bud Grant, it will no doubt be gray and covered
with snow, temperature in the high teens. In the icy stands
sit fans as hardened as he, exhaling frozen breath for eternity.
And there, behind one end zone, are five shirtless guys, their
stomachs wide, their breasts in need of a bra. Each wears a
homemade Viking helmet; two blow Viking horns. All have
purple and gold initials painted on their chests which, in
the correct order, spell VIKES. They too exhale frozen breath,
pass frozen wind. The soul of Grant cracks a brief smile, then
signals Joe Kapp to keep it on fourth-and-one.

Cold weather is the ultimate NFL fan stimulant. Dark
skies that pelt fields with sleet and ice stir the lust of fat
men dressed in home team jerseys and animal masks, as well
as those who fancy the classic topless look, chests and faces
smeared in home colors. The relation of winter to costume
fetishism has yet to be fully explored, especially where football is concerned. But it is clear, at an empirical level, that

*In 1998 the Vikings *did* do well outdoors, save for a loss in Tampa Bay.
But their biggest defeat that season came in the NFC Championship
Game . . . in the Metrodome. Grant's revenge?

cold climates inspire those who play NFL dress-up to strike poses unthinkable in Phoenix or even Miami.

In Pittsburgh, for instance, Steelers fans prefer the rough trade look—hard hat, boots, U.S. STEEL logos emblazoned like tattoos or branding marks. It is a doubly retro style: 1) it recalls the days of Pittsburgh's industrial might; and 2) it brings back the look made popular by the hard-hat member of the Village People. Indeed, to watch a row of Steelers fans yell and stomp as their team drives downfield is to see a raw dance line at work. Stuff a Steelers touchdown towel into each back pocket and the image crystalizes like a disco ball spinning above closed mills and polluted rivers. It's a color-ful scene that enlivens a drab sector of the Rust Belt.

Contrast this with the customs of Packers fans. Green Bay natives endure the coldest temperatures nature metes out, and they outlast those visiting teams that are unprepared for a late winter game on Lambeau Field. This is where Vince Lombardi devised his brilliant Sweep, Paul Hornung trailing a wall of Packer muscle. This is where Bart Starr beat the frozen Cowboys in the 1967 NFL Championship Game. Green Bay is an icy web from which few opponents escape. To them Titletown is Wounded Knee and My Lai combined. So how do Packers fans honor their heritage? By wearing yellow cheese wedges as hats.

The cheeseheads are considered to be among the more amiable fans in the league. Their pride in Wisconsin's dairy production is unquestioned, and doubtless each to a person is jovial, warm, sincere. Yet one cannot imagine Lombardi looking up to the stands and finding the humor in such a display. Of course, the cheeseheads should not be prisoners to a ghost, however great. But it does seem an odd progression from the Packers' dynastic period. What happened? Explanations are fleeting but theories abound. A postulation that has its adherents deals with the sticky issue of inbreeding. As with small towns everywhere, especially those where families are kept indoors by arctic cold, procreation is achieved within tiny interlocking circles. Thus it is inevitable, perhaps accidental, that relatives of various proximities mate in order to keep the town alive. But in Green Bay there is added incentive: season tickets. Since the Packers are the only show in town (the Bucks and the Brewers play in nearby Milwaukee), access to home games is a serious business. The best way to keep one's seats is to aggressively breed generations of Packers fans who will inherit the tickets, then breed, bequeath, and so on. This game of genetic Twister so mutated Green Bay's citizens that they now venerate their team's glorious past with large triangular party favors. Hence, cheeseheads.

A compelling theory, but does it then follow that *all* costumed fans are inbred? Try making that case in Cleveland's reactivated Dawg Pound. For years the Dawgs were the most rabid of Browns fans. They wore canine masks, hard hats (again), and threw Milk-Bone biscuits into the end zone after Browns touchdowns. They bayed like the semihuman hounds they portrayed, and no sensible person wandered near them.* They were Cleveland's avant-garde, less a result

---

*Home run king Henry Aaron was a high-profile exception, donning raincoat and sunglasses and barking with the Dawgs—an odd fact that raises the question: Have other members of Cooperstown patronized eccentric fan scenes? Did Babe Ruth run with the bulls in Pamplona? Was Bob Feller seen throwing bags of peanuts at midget wrestlers, nailing them with his trademark heat?

of sloppy genetics than a conscious effort to rouse the inner beast. The nastier and colder the weather, the more primal the Dawgs became. The NFL tried to rein them in, took away their Milk-Bones, threatened action should their conduct prove obscene. But the Dawgs refused to be silenced. In 1995, when Browns owner Art Modell decided he would move the team to Baltimore, the Dawgs were finally beaten. In Cleveland's remaining home games, they howled their disapproval until, ultimately, they were left whimpering in the parking lot, death scent in their masks. It was as if Modell had them put to sleep and sold to Vietnamese drive-thrus. The Pound was hosed down and closed indefinitely.

During Cleveland's fallow period, there was little for the Dawgs to do. They would not root for the Baltimore Ravens, their beloved Browns reduced to a Poe-inspired symbol. And there was no chance they would cheer on Ohio's remaining franchise, the Cincinnati Bengals (created by Paul Brown after he was fired by Modell). All they desired was that their tan symbol be restored, intact. A few scenarios cropped up, including one where the Indianapolis Colts would move to Cleveland and become the Browns, which would allow the Ravens to change their name to the Colts. But this was pure fantasy. The Dawgs had to wait until Cleveland settled its lawsuit against Modell, which it finally did to the tune of $11 million. The city also kept the rights to the Browns team name and colors, which came in handy once the league awarded Cleveland a new franchise to begin play in 1999. After several winters of privately honoring Browns legends (votive candles set in Alpo cans), the Dawgs emerged to reclaim their Pound.

No other animal/fan concept approached that of the Dawgs. Redskins fans had their own variation called the Hogs—burly guys in dresses sporting plastic pig snouts. While the Hogs backed three Super Bowl championship teams (under Joe Gibbs), they lacked the verve of Browns fanatics. Compared to the Dawgs, whose wardrobe and rites would have fascinated Breton, the Hogs were a modest creation, something Caligula might have conceived on an off-day. Plus, they operated in Washington, D.C., a city not known for its pounding winter storms. Hogs often flee at the first sign of frost; and if they are near Cleveland, they usually end up on hooks in many of that city's fine slaughterhouses. Outdoor winter theater is not for the weak nor the sane. And there are few cities where fans possess the talent and lunatic desire to mount Dawglike productions.

One would think that Broncos fans might stage diverting rituals. After all, their symbol, a crazy horse with nostrils flared, lends itself to direct interpretation, unlike the Dawgs-to-Browns, Hogs-to-Redskins abstract fare. Also, they enjoy that mile-high altitude, which, come winter, gives them leverage over the coldest outdoor scene—Cleveland included. Yet Broncos games are relatively staid when compared to other NFL sites. There are no pantomime horse routines, no twisting of horse themes from *Equus* or *The Godfather*, no Marlboro displays or "Rawhide" cracking of whips. Denver's natural advantage is routinely wasted, ignored; not even their back-to-back Super Bowl wins inspired a surge in end zone performance art. It seemed that Broncos supporters preferred traditional fanatic roles, and according to *The New York Times*, Mile High Stadium was considered a "hot spot" when it came to roguish fan behavior. So too Cincinnati and New England's Foxboro Stadium. Here, as elsewhere, the nearest fans come to expressing themselves in theatrical terms is through impromptu stagings of *A Clockwork Orange*.

Few venues boast a finer collection of droogs than New Jersey's Giants Stadium and Philadelphia's Veterans Stadium. Only hours apart and so alike in fan profiles, it's hard to decide which place offers the better horror show. On paper it's a toss-up: only those subjected to the fists and thrown bottles can really say for sure. Some give the edge to the Meadowlands, home to both the Giants and Jets, which doubles the traffic of heavy drinkers. So combustible are these fans that the league usually schedules only preseason games between the two teams (though they did meet during the 1999 regular season). Nothing is at stake save parking lot pissing rights; and once the obligatory matchup ends (hopefully with minor property damage), the regular season juggling of home games begins. Monday night contests are usually avoided for the simple reason that this will give fans of either team more time to get loaded. Before one Jets–Bills Monday night game, painters caps were given away as part of a promotional stunt. Before long, smoke billowed from parts of the stadium as Jets fans set fire to the caps with the intention, one later said, to read their team's future in the flames. It was there that the era of Parcells was presumably foretold, after which the fires were then extinguished in the standard drunken way.

But the Jets merely borrow Giants Stadium when the real home team travels or observes a bye week. They are forever the Mets to the Giants' Yankees, and since the Jets once played in Shea Stadium and the Giants in Yankee Stadium, it is a contrast that endures. Like their Yankee cousins, Giants fans act in an antisocial manner because for many it is the highest form of expression. Those who visit this strange and violent place are often amazed by the natives' behavior. Ross Greenburg, executive producer of HBO's "Real Sports," told *The New York Post* of the time he brought his wife and kids to see the Giants play the Cowboys. "A woman seated behind us was so drunk she vomited all over herself. Two men, right nearby, spent the entire game drinking and screaming obscenities. And my kids soaked all this up. They were scared. We're not going back, at least not with the kids. Actually, my wife won't go back either." Yet Greenburg's experience is mild when compared to the "Snowball Game" played in December 1995. Toward the end of a losing effort against the Chargers, Giants fans began hurling ice balls at San Diego personnel. It was fun pelting California assholes with spheres of Jersey ice. Even NBC was amused as its cameras focused away from the dull game and onto some of the better throws—one of which hit the Chargers' equipment manager, Sid Brooks, in the face, breaking his jaw, knocking him cold. Brooks could have been killed, but the rush was too pure for Giants fans to stop. Their missiles rained on the players through the final gun as everyone on field ran for the exits.

Brooks survived. (Thankfully, NBC caught the incident from a variety of angles and aired it, repeatedly, in slow motion.) But the home crowd's actions were a bit over the line for Meadowlands security officials. Some 175 fans were ejected and one publicly charged, a twenty-six-year-old Jersey man caught on videotape and put on the covers of New York's tabloids. He seemed a typical Garden State rube, but as John Samerjan of the New Jersey Sports and Exposition Authority told the press, not all of those ejected shared the same social status. "The extraordinary thing is who they are . . . It wasn't college kids who had too much beer. There was a middle-school principal and a retired police chief. People were claiming that everybody was doing it, but our security people were just shaking their heads and saying, 'Who *are* you?' "

That no one answered with a flurry of fists would suggest they weren't Eagles fans, for whom ejection from the Vet has long been a Sunday badge of honor. Even by Jets and Giants standards, Philly boosters are a nasty lot who routinely beat the piss out of unfortunate others, a fair amount of which splashes on still more drunks who take offense and join the fray. By the 1997 season, when the Eagles failed to improve upon the previous year's 10–6 record, many of these fine fellows were deemed officially "out of control." After a November 10 game against the 49ers, during which the off-field violence mirrored that of the players, the Philadelphia police warned fans that stricter rules would be in effect for the next home game against the Steelers. Apparently, a handful of those who attended that game never got the word or chose to ignore it. Twenty fans were rounded up for various acts of disorder and violence and taken to the cellar of Veterans Stadium. There they stood before Municipal Court Judge Seamus P. McCaffery, who found seventeen of the accused guilty of disturbing the peace. No books were thrown nor racks brought forth. The culprits were handcuffed, lectured to, fined, and videotaped. Many observers thought this a firm first step in the war against hooliganism. But if public embarrassment was the goal of those in charge, why not parade violators in front of Judge Judy?

It is commonly held that alcohol is to blame for much of the rowdiness at NFL games. The same is said of those home drinkers for whom Sundays and Monday nights are high times indeed. But is the violence that accompanies the drinking inspired by the game, or is it an innate part of the drinking fan himself? In most cases, it is usually a blend of both. After all, a man incapable of hitting another person will rarely do it while drunk, even if his brain is saturated with rib-cracking sacks, clothesline tackles, and flagrant spearings. But the man who knows and likes the feeling of striking others, preferably those who don't strike back, needs little encouragement when drinking. Thoughts of wicked sideline hits may help, but if committed to attack he will proceed regardless of the images in his head. This especially is true for the guy who beats his wife or girlfriend with the remote while beer chills on ice near his recliner. The game he watches is more soundtrack than stimulus, and after several beers and perhaps a few shots (Jagermeister and Bud blend nicely), he's ready to assert his dominance of home and flickering tube.

Battered women's shelters have for years cited Super Bowl Sunday as a day when complaints of abuse pour in. Like any other time, abuse is difficult to verify minus bruises, chipped teeth, broken bones. After all, it's her word against his, and oftentimes a woman will retract her complaint for fear that her husband/boyfriend will go to jail or become even angrier and kill her. But unless those who run the shelters are liars or the women who call in are overly dramatic and seeking attention, it may be that the season's final game brings out a few more beasts than normal. To make this publicly known, several groups bought commercial airtime during the 1994 Super Bowl and submitted a public service announcement that told women what they could do if abuse was a problem in their lives. The PSA aired. Reaction was swift. Primarily offended was Ken Ringle of *The Washington Post,* who believed that the Super Bowl itself was under attack. The assertion that women are beaten like AFC wild cards was a slander upon men and America. It was the junk sociology of PC fascism; an exercise in feminist castration. Ringle's piece was picked up and expanded on by various media, from the wise elders of *The Wall Street Journal*'s editorial page to Katharine Dunn, author of *Geek Love,* a story of romance among circus freaks. All viewed the PSA as specious. The possibility that there was *some* truth in the claims made by women's groups was simply dismissed. Meanwhile at NBC, which broadcast the Super Bowl that year, football analyst O. J. Simpson reportedly watched the abuse spot and said to a staffer, "That ain't shit. Man, you gotta hit 'em so hard they can't reach the phone!"

Not everyone who gets blasted on Super Sunday longs to smack their bitch up. Many just love the way football looks and sounds when they are drunk. It remains one of the better booze-enhanced spectator sports around, rivaled only by demolition displays, tractor pulls, dog fighting, and unregulated hand-to-hand combat. But football plays better to a drunk viewer's awareness. The pace of the game reflects the drinking ritual itself, from kickoff returns (first swig of a beer or cocktail), to sustained, run-oriented drives (steady pounding of twelve-ounce cans), to spectacular pass completions (chugging a bottle's last ounces), to the two-minute drill (running to the bathroom before losing bladder control). Then there's the simple pleasure of watching the players tear the raw humanity out of each other. One's central nervous system buzzes at such sights, a sensation intensified by the alcohol of choice. Beer, an obvious favorite, eases the fan into the mayhem and keeps him well lubricated throughout. Southern whiskey lends a yahoo edge to a one-yard gain. British gin amplifies on-field collisions. A martini per quarter raises the level of action to that of Japanese animation. By the fourth, even Billy Joe Hobert attains the grandeur of Akira.

When choosing vodka, the astute drinking fan prefers anything Russian over the Swedish, Finnish, and, certainly, American brands. At the premium end is Stoli, which, as the official drink of Russia's collapse, gives the fan a clean, vibrant high from where he may observe the breaking of bodies and—if lucky—of spirits. At the lower end are a host of unpronounceable brands that suggest distilled gasoline; yet, if taken slowly, any one will provide a nice Stoli-ish glaze. If thrown back like water, however, there is the risk of visions so extreme that it will take every fiber of sanity to keep you from torching your home, then running through the streets, stopping traffic.

Booze is a popular fan narcotic, pushed regularly on television and in magazines. But other chemicals go equally well with a variety of sports. Marijuana is perfect for baseball, especially when observing pitchers. Any Humbolt or Mendicino strain will take one directly into the strike zone, a once firm place that now shifts from inning to inning. A single hit from a frosted purple bud defines the outside and inside corners in ways that, should any umpire share your weed, would change the game for the better. Once the initial rush ebbs and perception sets in, you follow each pitch to the plate and admire the beauty of its arc, its rate of speed, its course, and its final location. It is a lovely thing to watch. You connect to the game at its purest level and explore its geometric properties as you would vivid blueprints of classical architecture.* Alcohol deadens this awareness and makes baseball another tribal contest.

The same is true of basketball. For years a game where speed was secondary to strategy (so much so that Converse's Chuck Taylor line was the sneaker of choice), basketball evolved in the early eighties as players grew (six-foot-nine-inch point guards) and the pace accelerated. Soon the fast break was the acme of the NBA offense, hanging jams the norm. Passes went cross court, three-pointers rained, and all became blurry as fans drank and drank and tried to keep up. Most inadequate. Because basketball shows no signs of slowing, its nuances are best caught and appreciated through either potent Cali herb or quality grade hashish. Lebanese blonde works as well as any black Tibetan variety one might acquire, and like smoking weed

---

*In his book *The Wrong Stuff*, "Spaceman" Bill Lee described his mound experiences after smoking pot and/or hash. The former Red Sox and Expos lefty took a physiological interest in the relation of chemicals to baseball and remains one of the game's more insightful observers.

to enjoy baseball, one should remain at home with one's water pipe and watch the sport on TV.

Under the mellow influence of hash, the NBA flow becomes clear: A minimum number of set plays gives the impression that the game is something more than forty-eight minutes of elevated street ball—which it is not. The improvisational nature of NBA play is its essence, a quality best appreciated by a mind glistening with THC. That ten large swift men running a ninety-foot rectangle control their movements with such dexterity is a delight to witness stoned. The look-away assists, the fluid pick-and-rolls, the baseline moves to the hole make one appreciate the circuitry in an athlete's brain and his ability to execute the orders transmitted when he faces a switch-off or is aggressively double-teamed. Hash peels back game faces to reveal the wiring within. Psilocybin does this too, but the colors are so intense and definition so acute that the wires appear as coral adders jutting from each player's face in a tangle of flickering tongues and venomous fangs. The court becomes a hardwood pit and the ball throbs in time to the snakes' hissing. This distracts from the game itself, which is why no serious basketball fan ingests psychedelics before tip-off.

Hallucinogens and sports occasionally mesh. Many native tribes ate peyote or hallucinogenic roots and plants in preparation for their respective games, including lacrosse and, sometimes, the torture and execution of enemy tribesmen, in its day considered a contact sport. Today it is the spectators who primarily trip (though a few pro jocks have played while under the influence—the infamous LSD no-hitter pitched by the Pirates' Dock Ellis, for instance). A reference to this practice was made in the golf comedy *Caddyshack*. A Park Avenue debutante, in an attempt to seduce Chevy Chase (Zen golfer), lists her hobbies, among them, watching bullfights on acid. It's a fleeting line that is tossed off and forgotten. But those who've actually *experienced* a bullfight while hallucinating would never be so blasé when speaking of it. Few things in this world affect one so profoundly as does this. It simply cannot be shaken.*

When it comes to violent American sports, the preferred

---

*In his 1977 travelogue, *Iberian Mindfields*, "a bevy of *tourista*-delic sights and sounds," Keith Susskind, known briefly as the "drugged-out Bruce Chatwin," described his bullfight-on-acid experience:

> The initial rush nearly drives you out of your seat as you await the introduction of the matador. You scan the stadium and notice you're the palest person there, a weak cell inside a healthy brown body. You then realize that your superego is dissolving as the energy of your being coalesces with the life forces around you. Oneness. You are the matador anticipating the bull's release and you feel agreeably tense. The bull storms out of his lair, stops, snorts, and glares at you with murderous eyes. His face changes shape and for a long moment you swear he's George Foreman with horns, his ears dripping flesh, his lower jaw weighed down by four rows of incisors. You steady yourself as he prepares to attack.
>
> The patterns in your cape swirl hypnotically and you hope this will mesmerize the beast. No luck. His body swells. His hide bubbles like hot cheese. His hooves kick up dust that he inhales like cocaine. His pupils dilate. You want to run but are frozen. He charges, heaving and panting and drooling yellow slime. You consider a variety of moves, and your brain spins off options as the bull nears. Finally, you decide. You pull your sword and drive it deep into the bull's throat. The sensation of steel cutting through flesh runs up your arm and saturates your left hemisphere. Orgasm dizziness. Dark crimson sprays, as though a sprinkler is attached to his neck. He staggers and gurgles. You hear laughter, but it is the sound of his jugular pumping life from his body. Sitting cross-legged next to his now crumpled frame, you watch blood spread like veins across the stadium's dirt floor. A white rose falls between you and the bull, its petals become wet and sticky red. You lift it to your nose and breathe in. Its scent takes you back to your seat, where, drenched in sweat, you collapse, only to awake hours later outside of the stadium, your wallet and shoes missing, your eyes sensitive to the faintest light.

hallucinogen is usually some Special K rave concoction, cut with enough speed to keep the visions going for hours. Like crack, this stuff has a nasty edge that locks the fan into the bloodiest spectacles while keeping a smile on his face. Younger fans do not use drugs to enhance the aesthetic features of their favored pastimes: They desire hyperdrive sensations, a techno-rush conditioned partly by their generational boredom and partly by video games that warp the concept of pain and brutality. A lucrative market exists where virtual combat makes real sports seem static and flat.* One of the more recent additions to the genre was NFL Blitz, a product of the Midway company that promised "a wretched assault on the sense of fair play." In Blitz there are "no rules, no refs, no mercy," and so the players are free to maim one another at will—the faster and more savage the hit, the more exciting the play. Blitz was approved by NFL Properties, the league's marketing arm, which felt that it emphasized pro football's main selling point, i.e., crushing violence independent of the game itself. Of course, Commissoner Paul Tagliabue and his associates would never be so coarse as to admit this; they are gentlemen, after all. In fact, when an ad touting Blitz featured Steelers QB Kordell Stewart drilling marching band members in the head with wicked spirals, the league asked Midway to drop its spot. The violence portrayed seemed too casual for the NFL's refined taste. Inflicting comas is serious business and should not be passed off as whimsical or cute.

---

*Arena football is a middle ground of sorts, a live version of a video game. Football for the busy fan: passing, hitting, little strategy.

On the other hand, boyish enthusiasm for brain-rattling hits is encouraged, and no one around the NFL plays this role with more gusto than John Madden. The former Raiders coach has made a sweet living out of celebrating the league's most brutal elements. Madden packages himself as one who appreciates working-class players, the guys who get muddy, who have bits of wet turf in their face masks, who scarf piles of fried meat and eggs before games. His annual All-Madden Teams are represented by many of football's average Joes. Against this blue-collar backdrop lie the twisted, crippled bodies of those who spend too much time in the trenches. Above them sits Madden, grin wide, arms waving about, appreciations rendered in his "Hey, that's me" style. Lest anyone doubt his affection for brutality (and the big bucks it generates), simply pop in a John Madden Football video game and marvel at the carnage. In one there is the command "Sack the QB, send him to the hospital!" An ambulance collects the battered quarterback so he may receive medical attention, but not before it runs over other players as it speeds off the field. In another version of the game, players are clotheslined and thrown on their heads, their unconscious frames littering bright computerized turf. In the commercials that promoted his wares, Madden surveyed the grisly action and said, "You gotta laugh!" All the way to the bank, big guy.

Madden has been pretty honest about his intentions. He's not one to wring hands over the crippling aspects of football and then cash in on same; it's a straight deal all down the line. The cheery face he brings to the violence is mere showbiz panache. ("You gotta sell!" as he might say.) Recall that

Madden once coached a sadist named Jack Tatum, who before he became a Raider played under the demented glare of
Woody Hayes at Ohio State. There Tatum learned that football is about punishing and humiliating your enemy as thor-
oughly as possible. If you can knock him out of the game,
do it. This philosophy played well in Oakland as Madden
and his boss Al Davis took full advantage of Tatum's brutality. It was a Tatum hit that helped secure the Raiders' first
Super Bowl win in 1977. Early in the third quarter of that
game the Vikings trailed Oakland 19–7; but Minnesota's offense, led by Fran Tarkenton, put on an impressive drive and
it looked as if they would soon close the gap to five points.
When Tarkenton threw to Sammy White, Tatum clocked the
Vikings' receiver so hard that White's helmet popped off his
head and White, dazed beyond reason, was forced to leave
the game. That killed Minnesota's drive and their chances
for victory.

The hit on White, however, was an air-kiss compared to
what Tatum did to Darryl Stingley on August 12, 1978. In
an exhibition game against the Patriots, Tatum decided he'd
send a "message" to Stingley, one of New England's better
wide receivers. Tatum accomplished his mission, smashing
Stingley with such force that the former Purdue All-American
suffered a damaged spinal cord, his neck broken in two
places. Stingley hovered near death and survived as a quad-
riplegic. Tatum's response? He was just doing his job. Indeed, so proud was Tatum that he had a book written for
him, *They Call Me Assassin,* in which his style of football
was explained and naturally justified. The downside to all

this was that Tatum played in the wrong era. Were he active today, he would command a regal salary and be offered a slew of endorsement deals. Cutting-edge ads would glorify his cruelty and millions of kids would adore him. Following Madden's lead, Tatum would be given his own video game line: Assassin 2000, Blood Assassin 2001, Torture Freak Assassin 2002, "where *you* sever spinal columns with BONE-BREAKING HITS and fracture skulls with FLYING HELMET SLAMS . . ." Tatum's gritty play would also win him a spot on the All-Madden Team, " 'cause here's a guy who doesn't mind gettin' his uniform dirty! Hey, you gotta love that!"

Were Tatum truly great, he would have crippled some fans as well. In a way, his legacy is incomplete. Of course, no one will ever approach Ty Cobb, whose penchant for charging the stands remains unparalleled. He once savagely beat a man with no hands (but then the man had called Cobb a "half-nigger" and Dixie honor was to be avenged) and thought nothing of assaulting those fans, especially if black, who failed to pay him due respect. Today there are a few pretenders to Cobb's throne: tense Mike Tyson, Lawrence Phillips (product of Tom Osborne's Nebraska Finishing School for Gentlemen), and of course Charles Barkley, who cannot enjoy a private drink in peace. Yet none have the lunatic gleam that fans and opponents saw in Cobb's eyes. (Well, maybe Tyson.) It seems, however, that the fan has assumed the traditional role of sports nutcase—at least that's the message being sent into pop culture. Images of crazed fans saturate print, television, and film, and amid the clutter two distinct archetypes can be seen: the lovable obsessed nerd with no life and the unlovable obsessed nerd on the brink of a psychotic freakout.

This latter type served as centerpiece to the Tony Scott film *The Fan,* which could also have been titled *Travis Bickle Heads West.* Robert De Niro plays Gil Renard, a devoted San Francisco Giants fan whose van is a rolling advertisement for the team. We know from the start that Gil is unbalanced as he drives to the strains of "Sympathy for the Devil." And we see that he has chosen the newest Giant, Bobby Rayburn (Wesley Snipes), as the target of his obsession. The film deals with a few fan concerns—an average guy indentifying with a multimillionaire jock, the early despair of what looks to be a mediocre season, the placing of team loyalty over familial responsibilities. We get Rayburn's view of "die-hard fans" as "losers," to which Gil replies, "Without people like me, you're nothing!" But soon *The Fan* becomes a stalker flick as Gil's last threads of sanity snap amid the chaos of his life. Since Gil sells cheap hunting supplies, he conveniently has access to a variety of knives, which he wields with true artistry (perhaps his one real talent). He butchers several people along the way, including a teammate of Rayburn's who is enjoying a better year than the celebrity slugger and so must die. Gil finally eats lead as a heavy rain drenches 3Com Park. He is dressed in umpire's garb, which allows the film to end on that classic fan line "Kill the ump!"

As compelling as *The Fan* might have been, it does little to explore sports obsession. The film lacks a sense of humor, something that many real-world psychos possess, even though they alone understand the joke. Another film, *Celtic*

Pride, attempts to make fan lunacy funny, and while it does not quite hold up, it is in a modest way more frightening than *The Fan.* A gym coach Mike O'Hara (Daniel Stern) and his plumber friend Jimmy Flaherty (Dan Aykroyd) share a blind allegiance to Boston's pro teams, especially the Celtics. Each is a basket case of superstitious tics and customs, and come playoff time their conditions grow worse. When we meet Mike and Jimmy, they are hoping for a final Celtic championship in old Boston Garden. So great is their intensity that when the Jazz come to town to play the Celtics in the NBA Finals, the pair abduct Utah's leading scorer, Lewis Scott (Damon Wayans), and keep him bound to a chair in Mike's memorabilia-lined basement. Eventually Scott escapes, and rather than turn his kidnappers over to the police, he forces them to appear in the Garden for Game 7, wearing Utah jerseys. Through humiliation comes clarity as Mike and Jimmy learn a valuable lesson about fanaticism—at least when it comes to the Celtics. As for the Patriots, however . . .

Though a bit on the dopey side, *Celtic Pride* does have its moments. Daniel Stern's Mike is much scarier than De Niro's Gil simply because he is believable. And the observations made by Damon Wayans as he surveys his temporary cell are remarkably pointed and precise: Jimmy holds a gun on Scott; but it is Scott who fires with both barrels. He nods to a photo of Larry Bird on the wall and lets Jimmy have it:

> *It's pathetic. All these pictures of other people's achievements. What have you done? What's your claim to fame? You think Larry Bird has a picture of*

you *on his wall, with your hand down a toilet, wran-
gling a turd? He doesn't even know you exist . . . You
might as well take that gun and just put it in your
mouth and blow your brains out.*

Written by Judd Appatow before he composed his mas-
terpiece of criminal obsession, *The Cable Guy, Celtic Pride*
locates the germ of excessive fandom and exposes it to light.
The film's unevenness does it in, but its theme served ESPN
well when the network created "Rick," an *über*fan detached
from objective reality, clad in a Boston Bruins jersey and
devoted solely to twenty-four hours of sports programming.
As did MTV with Beavis and Butt-head, ESPN used Rick to
spoof its core audience while promoting shows that appealed
to same. Viewers equally devoted to the network either felt
that Rick respresented the fan next door or were simply flat-
tered by their reflection. While some sports observers have
bemoaned such pandering (most consistent among them Phil
Mushnick of *The New York Post,* about whom more later), it
does, at least in the short term, work. Those who conceive
the marketing campaigns know that the average fan believes
he is in some way *connected* to his favorite team and that
his obsession somehow contributes to the effort.

Many teams exploit this shamelessly in their PR efforts
and at times are lightly reprimanded by their respective
leagues. The NHL, for instance, expressed its "concern" with
the New York Islanders organization after it marketed its
1998 season as "Fighting Without Ear Biting" and told the
team's fans that soon "getting the barbecue started won't be

the only way of expressing your masculinity." Like the NFL and the video games that bear its seal, the NHL "officially" condemns abject brutality—but does little to prevent it at ice level, nor discourage it in the seats. The league did complain to Fox Sports during the '98 season when the network glorified brawls in its commercials, but nothing was done. As Fox spokesman Vince Wladika explained at the time, "We've promoted hockey for four years in many ways, but they didn't boost ratings. So we thought, 'Let's go back to the basic instinct and see if it works.' " Why not? After all, fans expect fisticuffs with their hockey and pay good money to see it. Give them what they desire. What are we, Finland?

3

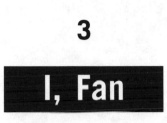

I, Fan

I'm not too thrilled with the sports media people either. The talent is marginal, they bring nothing to the mix, and their palpable envy of the players is actually embarrassing . . . You wanna know the problem? Athletes get tons of money and pussy, and all the best drugs. The sports media don't.

—GEORGE CARLIN

Guuuuh!

—KEITH OLBERMANN

Above the average fan sits the connoisseurs—fans who are paid to express their views to those down below. They understand sports more deeply than the commoners, appreciate the finer points of games like few around them. The professional fan operates in various forums but is never far from the amateur's sight. For without someone to enlighten or correct, the point to his or her professionalism is lost and each becomes as common as the rest. This is most evident in sports radio, where talk show hosts are once removed from those who phone them. The typical host is white, male, heavyset, obsessive, egomaniacal, brusque. His opinions are many, his imagination limited. His age is anywhere from early thirties to mid-fifties. If he is at all political, he will tend to be rightist, in some cases reactionary. And like most reactionaries, he will portray himself as both maverick and victim, his views too strong for the wimp majority to digest.

The average radio host provides a place where fans of varying knowledge and intensity may deliver their assessments of recent games, individual performances, trade rumors, and so on. Some callers are amiable and wish only to add their two cents. Others blast the host for his purported ignorance, arrogance, and flacking on behalf of the unpopular figure of the moment: owner, high-salaried player not performing as expected, manager or coach, whose decisions leave local fans fuming. This doesn't happen as often as it should; yet when it does, it becomes an odd battle of wills, oftentimes reduced to an ad hominem exchange of stats and dates. The irate caller is rarely intimidated by the host and will push his case to the limit. But since the host controls the microphone and the switchboard, he always has the final word, which usually serves as crude punch line.

Every town and city has some type of sports radio programming; but it is in the bigger venues where the real "characters" are heard. In New York, the country's largest market, there is the all-sports station WFAN and its top act, "Mike and the Mad Dog"—Mike Francesa and Chris Russo. Each is incomparably Noo Yawk in accent and demeanor, and this means that listeners get an earful of know-it-all bravado as the pair dissect local teams and the national scene with equal fervor. As radio hosts go, Francesa and Russo are relatively polite to those who call in, most of whom, of course, are in need of swift correction. Francesa has gone solo on occasion, most prominently when he appeared on CBS to analyze the NCAA basketball tournament. He seemed out of place sitting between the sedate Jim Nantz and the hyper Bill Raftery (who becomes even stranger when calling Nets games), and he often picked the wrong team to win its respective bracket. As prognosticator Francesa has not been terribly keen, but then neither has his partner, Russo. Yet the two are attentive to the stratagems of New York's various clubs and dispense some truly arcane information to their listeners, a loyal, vocal lot.*

Indeed, it is the arcane that sends sports radio listeners to the phones, if nothing more than to flaunt their grasp of minutiae. One often hears a flurry of obscure references made during a typical radio hour, and in this sense sports talk is more democratic, hence more interesting, than its political cousin. As the noted linguist (and Celtics fanatic) Noam Chomsky has observed, some of those who call sports radio shows are unusually independent-minded when stressing their points. They use their cognitive abilities to break down a coach's strategy, dismiss the excuses given after a favored team's loss as so much propaganda. In other words, they rely on their own intelligence to make determinations in spite of what a host might say to deter them.

By contrast, many who call political radio shows spew out jargon that a bright eighth grader would find absurd. That they are egged on by hosts who are, by and large, fascistic makes political radio a form of audio theater that amuses but does not inform. Sports radio, on the other hand, offers a wide range of data that one may pick through and examine

---

*Francesa, however, tends to get too chummy with those he is paid to assess—specifically Bill Parcells—and this naturally warps his judgment when he discusses the Jets. Russo, too, part of the Jets combine in 1998, hosting a postgame show with former Jet and Redskin, John Riggins.

at leisure. The reason for this, says Chomsky, is that people are encouraged to spend their time assessing stats and figures that have nothing to do with the real world. Sports are reserved for the credulous mass; politics the educated few. So instead of studying history and assessing contemporary events, fans use their brains to ponder whether the Dolphins should have gone for it on fourth-and-two or if the Astros might shuffle the top of their order to better their chances of early inning runs. But even contemplative fans are now shoved aside by the sports world's lower orders. And, predictably, radio and television play to this by featuring hosts who thrive on sensation.

Jim Rome is one. Rome began his sports radio career in San Diego and later gained notoriety as a raucous host in Los Angeles. His smart-ass tone caught the attention of ESPN, which hired Rome to host a chat show on its smaller outlet, ESPN2, where, in 1994, he made his mark. While interviewing Rams quarterback Jim Everett, Rome repeatedly referred to him as "Chris Evert," since he was, in Rome's eyes, a girl unworthy of his male name. Everett warned Rome to stop. Rome kept calling him "Chris." Everett then threw aside the table that separated them and went after Rome, the result being a standard TV altercation: a studio hand rushing between the two, lapel mikes smothered and scraped against clothing, disorder captured on three cameras. The event was replayed nationwide and so brought Rome's smirking face (and backpedaling form) to millions of viewers who did not watch "The Deuce," ESPN2's "hip" moniker. Rome later apologized to Everett and Evert (for trivializing the tennis great's abilities), but his reputation was made among fans who saw themselves as outlaws in the Rome mold.

Rome developed a core following among fans who became known as "clones," a fitting tag, as they are slavishly devoted to their hero.* When they call Rome's radio show, "The Jungle," the clones are told to "have a take and don't suck" if they are to remain on-air with the Master. Instead of challenging Rome or offering fresh insights, the clones must keep the pace alive and mimic the verbal stylings of the host. (According to the show's producer, Travis Rodgers, the concept of the caller "as guest" is past.) The vocabulary used is termed "gloss" for glossary, and is made up, Rodgers says, of "East Coast jargon, ghetto jargon, California surfer talk" among other exotic dialects. This is where the "Chris Evert" slur originated, for Rome and his clones use the locker room and prison yard tactic of feminizing those beneath their contempt (e.g., "Christine" for Christian Laettner, because he has "fair" features and whines like a chick). When appraising female athletes, the clones employ the trusty "pig" as all-purpose insult, though sometimes, if a woman's features are rodentian, she will be listed with the "rats," sports figures who possess that squinty, squeaky look—Monica Seles, for one.

Rome, or "Romey" as he is called by his followers, plays fantasy rebel leader to those who believe that phoning a

---

*On the televised version of his radio show, Fox Sports Net's "The Last Word," Rome refers to his onscreen audience as "peeps," who hoot and wail on cue while Rome smirks and does his trademark shtick. Rome's contempt for his East Coast fans has been publicly expressed, but only on the West Coast, where the "peeps" cannot see or hear his put-downs.

sports radio show constitutes some level of defiance. It's quite a profitable racket, and one can hardly blame Rome (or his backers) for cashing in. But Rome is not the only syndicated host who walks this beat. Opposing him in many markets is Nanci Donnellan, known to her fans as "The Fabulous Sports Babe" (or "Blob" in Rome-gloss, a dig at her considerable heft). The Babe does not, she says, "suffer fools lightly." She abuses those who call in and fail to show her the proper respect. Donnellan is the only woman who hosts a national sports show of any kind, a niche she exploits rather loudly. While she paints herself as an opera and jazz devotee, Donnellan flogs sports with dominatrix abandon, thrashing the hide off anything that irks her. As with Rome, analysis and appreciation are drowned out by the commotion. Rick Scott, a programming consultant for sports radio, said it best to *The New York Times*: "Nobody cares about X's and O's. It's not about information; it's about opinion and a unique perspective. The Babe's got a real grasp on the entertainment aspect."

Although one can hear Donnellan on nearly 190 ABC Radio affiliates, her "unique perspective" was captured for posterity in a book, *The Babe in Boyland*. As the title infers, the Babe's story is about a woman who goes up against male odds to become the "#1 nationally syndicated sports radio talk show host" in the U.S.A. Once she reaches this peak, she looks down on her male competitors as "boys stewing in their own testosterone who don't know anything beyond eating pizza, jerking off, and playing Fantasy Football."

While she ostensibly does none of the above (at a glance, it seems she has eaten her share of pizza), the Babe can be as crude as the boys she scorns.

Throughout the book, a variety of jocks, owners, executives, and cities are told to blow her and get fucked, their trangressions ranging from greed to stupidity to sexism. The Babe comes down hard on many athletic psychopaths like Mike Tyson and Lawrence Phillips, but has a soft spot for Don King: "Yes, he once beat a man to death. Yes, he ripped off a stable of fighters for the lion's share of their winnings. Yes, he used up, and then sold out, Muhammad Ali." Yet he "saved boxing," so his misdeeds, while serious, are relatively minor when compared to his keeping alive a sport that made him rich at the expense of dazed boxers with birds tweeting around their heads. The Babe likes King "because he's always a great guest on the show, one who's never afraid to be completely wack." While "wack" is good for ratings, does she expect anything less from the flashy ex-con?*

The Babe's book was "written" (in tandem with Neal Karlen) to approximate her speech patterns, much in the same manner of Howard Stern's *Miss America* and Dennis Rodman's *As Bad As I Wanna Be*. And like these fine volumes, the layout is a RIOT of different 𝓕𝓞𝓡𝓣𝓢 and letter points, *italicized* *bursts*, and other editorial gimmicks to hold the attention of those who find traditional

---

*The Babe could make the same case for O. J. Simpson, whom she righteously deplores: "Yes, he murdered his ex-wife and her friend. Yes, he played down and excused his abuse of Nicole. Yes, he portrayed himself as a helpless victim of police harassment and racism. Yet he was one of the best running backs the NFL has ever seen, as well as an effective and trusted pitchman . . ."

print rough going. Ultimately, it was her bosses at ESPN Radio, where she first received national exposure, who blanched at many of her comments. During her first six months with the network, some ESPN "Goober in a suit with a big attitude would be in the studio every day telling me this, bitching about that . . . But I stood my ground and told all the suits to please get out of my airstream. If they hadn't, I swear to Jesus I would have gotten Uzis and sandbagged the radio booth." The Babe so ridiculed her employers that after the book was released in 1996, she was as well. ABC Radio then hitched her to its syndicated wagon and the Babe has pulled in ratings and profits ever since.

The Babe and Jim Rome are exceptions in sports radioland. Each is artfully bombastic enough to draw listeners who wish to share their heat, and each has the syndicated muscle to ensure widespread renown. Most sports radio hosts dwell in local and regional hell where, like hamsters on a treadmill, they are expected to concentrate solely on local teams (which is, many GMs insist, the backbone of sports radio). Since the early nineties, however, moves have been made to syndicate not just a particular personality but an entire roster of characters—twenty-four hours of sports chat and game coverage packaged for your convenience. ESPN Radio made its bid in 1992, and to date has more than 420 affiliates under its banner. But ESPN, for all its wise guy rep (owed mostly to the televised "SportsCenter"), is rather bland when compared to other outlets: just ask the Babe. A newer, brasher network has emerged over the past several years and it, unlike staid ESPN, is devoted to making as much foul noise as is legally permissible. One-On-One Sports operates in Northbrook, Illinois, a suburb north of Chicago. It is the product of Chris Brennan, the network's president and CEO. Brennan came to the logical conclusion that as "the world gets smaller, more people want to know what's going on in the world." Going against received wisdom, Brennan believed that a "local sports-talk station can be almost too myopic. After the twenty-fifth Yankee call in a row, it starts to get montonous."

So in 1994 Brennan assembled a roster of hosts and syndicated it nationwide. By 1998, One-On-One Sports was heard in 385 markets, including Boston, Los Angeles, New York, and Chicago, where Brennan acquired and reformatted ailing stations, then went head-to-head with those cities' established sports outlets. As he put it, "We're not looking for instantaneous results; it's a grass-roots effort. It's a slow build to establish personalities." Like the successful acts of Rome and the Babe, One-On-One's hosts place entertainment value over information, though if one listens long enough, some analysis trickles through the din. Each host plays his favorite brand of music as he rants about the day's sports news and scores (the sounds range from funk to soul to classic rock), and each enlists the callers to be actors in his specific slot. The emphasis is on velocity. As of this writing, One-On-One's line-up included the "opinionated, colorful, controversial" figure of Jay Mariotti (could he be anything less?), followed by afternoon host Peter Brown, a "provocative . . . watch dog for sports fans," as he's billed, and who, naturally, always "touches a nerve." In the evening, there is "Papa Joe" Chevalier who, while older than his fellow One-On-Oners, has fans who are as childish as those heard throughout the day. Papa Joe elicits "Bite me!" calls, a series of screams and spiteful comments intended as criticism of coaches, players, owners. Papa Joe listens attentively, then adds his views which, let us say, would not be deemed gauche in certain militia circles. Arnie Spanier, a "bullhorn pointed at the sports world," guides listeners into late night, keeping them alert and alive as he "shouts, hurls and pitches his free-wheeling opinions" into the ether. And around the clock it goes. From the maladjusted to the heavily-caffeinated, One-On-One keeps fans' knees jerking.

Just above the radio hosts are the sportswriters, some of whom moonlight in broadcasting but most of whom make their livings in print. Sportswriting was once a noble art; writers who were not strictly sports fanatics composed beautiful essays and books about the games and figures that enthralled them. Such authors as P. G. Wodehouse, James Thurber, and Ring Lardner brought to life their favorite pastimes with true skill and appreciation. Although Wodehouse, who wrote of golf, and Thurber, who wrote of baseball, live on thanks to small devoted cults that celebrate their art, Lardner has pretty much fallen off the map. His prose, especially in *You Know Me, Al: A Busher's Letters Home,* a baseball tale set in the days of Ty Cobb and Honus Wagner, seems awkward at first glance. But Lardner's gift for capturing the slang of his time reminded many of his peers, H. L. Mencken and Virginia Woolf among them, of that master of plain

American speech, Mark Twain. His characters Jack "The Busher" Keefe and the hard-hitting Alibi Ike, known for waving off a manager's signal, then concocting an elaborate defense to excuse it, provide a glimpse into a world long dead. (He also enjoyed sitting with the fans, or "bugs" as he called them, for it was there Lardner felt a true appreciation for the game that at times seemed absent in the press box.) Those who are willing and able to read Lardner's stories will receive a lesson in history and in literature. Those who cannot are advised to rent *Eight Men Out*, John Sayles's account of the 1919 Black Sox scandal in which the director himself plays Lardner, a sly wit wearing a straw boater who is wise to the fix early on.

Since baseball is our oldest game, it has been interpreted by generations of scribes. Its idyllic quality brings out the poet in even the toughest observer, so powerful is its influence, its myth. Lardner and Thurber have been noted. John Updike, who has written about everything from New England witches, suburban adultery, Wasp malaise, Jewish anxiety to the end of the world, delivered elegant takes on the sport, the most celebrated of which was "Hub Fans Bid Kid Adieu," his first-person account of Ted Williams's final game in Fenway Park.

Updike captures the atmosphere in his trademark, lilting prose; and when Williams stepped to the plate for the last time, Updike takes perhaps the fullest picture of that classic at-bat. Facing a one-one pitch from the Orioles' Jack Fisher, Williams swung, connected, and "there it was." The ball shot into the "vast volume of air over center field." To Updike, the ball seemed not to fly but formed the tip of "a towering, motionless construct," an Eiffel Towering home run. Williams circled the bases (like "a feather caught in a vortex") as he always did after slamming a homer: full-out. The fans, Updike included, went crazy, but Williams never looked up nor acknowledged their praise.

Back in the Red Sox dugout, Williams ignored the fans' pleas to emerge and take a bow. His fellow players, the umpires as well, urged Williams to emerge and at least tip his hat. He refused. "Gods do not answer letters," observed Updike. Today, lesser souls eagerly fill this gap.

Updike's 1960 piece appeared in *The New Yorker,* whose editor at the time, William Shawn, published some of the better sportswriting seen during the postwar, pre-Vietnam years. When it came to the Grand Old Game, however, no one in the magazine could touch Roger Angell, whose essays should be read by anyone who fancies himself a "real" baseball fan.

Angell's descriptive talent is what first hits you, the way he casually but fully establishes a scene. But like all fine writers it is in nuance and shade where Angell achieves full effect. Musing on the demolition of New York's famous Polo Grounds, home to the Giants and briefly the Mets, Angell's memory takes him back to "sights and emotions so inconsequential that they will surely slide out of my recollection." Pigeons flying from "the barn shadow" of the Grounds' upper stands, into right field and swooping above the "inert, heat-heavy flags on the roof"; the sound of a line drive hitting the wooden barrier above the left-field stands; one's arm resting on a chain in the box seats, the "sun-warmed iron" felt through one's shirtsleeve; night games, with the moon, resembling a "spongy, day-old orange balloon," rising above the scoreboard, highlighting the clouds of cigarette smoke hanging over the seats.

But Angell, for all his thoughts of ballparks past, is no soft nostalgist. He has always been realistic, if mournful, about baseball's ultimate destination. In the early 1970s, after monuments to bad design were erected in Cincinnati, Pittsburgh, and Philadelphia, and the game itself became corporatized, Angell accurately gauged where baseball, as well as all pro sports, was heading. The American sports obsession, while not new, had by that time become known for its "excessive excessiveness." What *was* new, as Angell saw it, was a "curious sense of loss"; the loss of each game's uniqueness where players seemed larger than life, where they displayed a kind of courage and style that set one sport apart from the next. These singular achievements and special joys had, at the time of Angell's essay, disappeared, lost "somewhere in the noise and crush."

Noise and crush now rule so much of the culture that sport resembles other forms of entertainment, including national politics. Special joys have no place except as marketing tools. Seasons are practically meaningless. Angell assumed that even casual fans would be unsettled by these events, which shows he had faith in the American fan's traditionalist instincts. He was wrong, at least when it came to the majority that happily assembled in ghastly concrete saucers to watch baseball played on faded carpets. This was

progress, they were told, and who knew any differently?*
Angell certainly knew this was inevitable and he gently
railed against something he could do nothing about. He later
noted that his indignation stemmed from innocence, that he
had yet to clearly see the mercenary side of pro sports. He
got the picture soon enough and has remained focused ever
since; we live, after all, in an age of no surprises. But Angell's
early work was anything but innocent. It was a living guide
to the promise of spring, the march through summer, the
race to fall. He honored and gave voice to the myth. Reading
Angell's work from that period takes one to the final days of
genuine ball, complete with fan noise, bleacher smells, and
transistor radios. His appreciations stand alone, and one
wonders who among today's crop of scribes will pen the
eulogy when the Astrodome is demolished.

Baseball's only rival for the hearts and minds of writers
has been boxing. There are as many prose poems dedicated
to men in blood-splattered trunks as there are for those who
hit home runs or pitch no-hitters. Boxing is a curious sport,
primal and very American. It has always appealed to the
working class, those beer-soaked boys who relish a good fight
from a safe distance (save for the occasional fan melee in the
ring, like the one that followed Andrew Golata's punch to
Riddick Bowe's crotch in Madison Square Garden). Here boxing cuts across racial lines and the mayhem is equally en-

---

*Some twenty-plus years later, new parks, like Jacobs Field in Cleveland
and Camden Yards in Baltimore, were built in answer to the above mon-
strosities. An improvement of sorts, but these type of parks, a "homage"
to the classic fields of yesteryear, are to the original articles as linoleum is
to mahogany—shopping malls with a human face.

joyed. But as we work our way ringside we see fewer dark faces taking in a savage twelve-rounder. Many white-collar types drawn to boxing love the rearrangement of flesh and bone as much as, if not more than, those in the cheap seats behind them. They really enjoy watching the lesser breeds beat the living shit out of each other. But how do these civilized voyeurs justify their attraction to so primitive a spectacle? Not only to themselves but to each other?

One way is to describe fighting in classical terms. This was Joyce Carol Oates's strategy in her piece, *On Boxing*. Oates, who writes on average six to eight books a year along with thousands of essays, has a wide range of interests. Boxing is one. Physically, Oates is slight, but she feeds heavily on the sight of big black men engaged in violent struggle. Still, she wouldn't put it as plainly as this. "I don't 'enjoy' boxing in the usual sense of the word, and never have," she writes. "[B]oxing isn't invariably 'brutal,' and I don't think of it as a 'sport.'" If not a sport, then what? "Each boxing match is a story—a unique and highly condensed drama without words . . . Boxers are there to establish an absolute experience, a public accounting of the outermost limits of their beings . . . To enter the ring near-naked and to risk one's life is to make of one's audience voyeurs of a kind: Boxing is so intimate. It is to ease out of sanity's consciousness and into another, difficult to name. It is to risk, and sometimes to realize, the agony of which *agon* (Greek 'contest') is the root."

Too bad Mike Tyson's attorney didn't dig this up when his client sought the restoration of his license. The line about boxers easing "out of sanity's consciousness and into another, difficult to name" fits Tyson perfectly. Better still, he could have put Oates on the stand as a character witness: *"Every talent must unfold itself in fighting.* So Nietzsche speaks of the Hellenic past, the history of the 'contest' . . . and so might he have spoken of Mike Tyson, whose own 'will to power' would doubtless have impressed the late German philosopher, as well as the Greeks, if not the Romans, all of whom would pay top dollar to see Mike fight under the bright lights of Vegas . . ." A prime opportunity missed for Oates to state her nonbrutal sport theory on behalf of an ear-biting rapist. Yet despite her classical allusions (but no metaphors, for "boxing really isn't a metaphor, it is the thing in itself"), Oates cannot hide the fact that she likes to watch the blood fly and the bodies fall. She especially heats up when tracing the history of gladitorial combat, then gives away the game in a revealing passage: "While it is plausible that emotionally effete men and women may require ever more extreme experiences to arouse them, it is perhaps the case, too, that the desire is not merely to *mimic* but, magically, to *be* brute, primitive, instinctive, and therefore innocent."

George Plimpton has tried to find such innocence. In *Paper Lion* he described his time in camp with the Detroit Lions, his ultimate goal to run an offensive series in a preseason scrimmage. The results were comical, of course; Plimpton's gangly frame and inability to handle the snaps made him bad quarterback material, but his experience resulted in a book and subsequent film (starring Alan Alda as Plimpton), which was, after all, the point to the whole exercise. Plimpton also tried his hand at boxing, going three rounds against Archie Moore, the former light heavyweight champion. He wrote of this encounter in *Shadowbox,* and it too has its humorous qualities. (As part of his training, Plimpton reads an Olde English book on the gentlemen's art of prizefighting.) For unlike Joyce Carol Oates, whose attraction to the ring is so intense that were she to lace on gloves her inner brute would emerge and no one would be safe, Plimpton's approach to boxing was more in the line of "I say, here's a lark: me, in trunks, trading blows with a black man!" His account of the fight, and the training that led up to it, lacks any serious edge. Plimpton is smart enough to be self-deprecating about his physique and ability to fight, and there is all along a winking certainty that our George is never in danger. (The worst he suffers is a bloody nose.) Plimpton writes of Moore in pleasant terms, as would a benevolent master of a strong but loyal manservant: "His face was peaceful, with a kind of comforting mien to it . . . and to be put away by him in the ring would not be unlike being tucked in by a Haitian mammy." Well put, old boy!

At the opposite end of the ring stands Norman Mailer. Like Oates, Mailer has explained his love of fighting in layers and layers of prose, some of which is quite impenetrable. Like Plimpton, he has mixed it up in seedy gyms. But where Oates affected detachment and Plimpton played Ichabod Crane among beasts, Mailer paid religious homage to those who mete out the pain. Of course today Mailer is less animated about the joys of violence, advanced age being a significant factor. But in the sixties and seventies when he was a rapid-fire proponent of masculinity and male pride, Mailer saw it as every man's duty to release his primal self from the shackles of femininity and feminism. Or to put it in Mailerspeak: a pussy is something you fuck, not something you are. So it was no shock that Mailer found in boxing the answers to many probing questions about male existence and man's connection to his inherent brutality. He also saw boxing as a linguistic construct. "There are languages other than words," he wrote in *Existential Errands* (which came out the same year, 1975, as his report on the Ali-Foreman bout in Zaire, *The Fight*), "languages of symbol and languages of nature. There are languages of the body. And prizefighting is one of them."

Far from speaking a language of mere grunts, boxers, Mailer tells us, speak "with a command of the body which is as detatched, subtle, and comprehensive in its intelligence as any exercise of mind by such social engineers as Herman Kahn or Henry Kissinger." This is indeed flattering. Imagine a fighter whose punch packs the same force as a winnable nuclear war, Kahn's unfulfilled dream, or who lays out his opponent with a series of blows that recall the saturation bombing of Southeast Asia, one of Dr. K's contributions to civilization. To the untrained eye, such a "dialogue between bodies" might seem riotous or brash. But, as Mailer points out, these are "*conversational* exchanges which go deep into the heart of each other's matter." Fighters, "[i]gnorant men, usually black, and usually next to illiterate, address one another" this way. They "stick with the wit their bodies provide . . . They talk with many a silent telepathic intelligence." Mailer deciphered these conversations for his fellow white boxing fans and used them to make sociological points. And as entertaining as he sometimes is in translation, one pictures an ignorant black fighter, taut body brimming with wit and telepathy, clocking Mailer in midrant, knocking him and his theories on their ass.

No writer ever painted boxing in the same colors as A. J. Liebling. A true virtuoso who wrote appreciatively of wine and scathingly of press barons, Liebling elevated the fight game through his prose but never lost the liniment-and-spit bucket immediacy of old gyms. He penned his essays for *The New Yorker*; and while William Shawn was put off by the whole bloody enterprise, Liebling's takes on prize-fighting were so direct and beautifully composed that they fit the magazine's mix throughout the 1950s and into the 1960s. Liebling pushed no grand theories, did not look for ways to sanitize the brutality of the sport. He provided his readers scenes of human hope and weakness, got close to the people who not only fought but also taped fists and mopped floors. He was, like the "New Journalists" who would succeed him, at the center of every story. But unlike some of his journalistic heirs, Liebling did not hog the spotlight. His was a light presence, someone who seemed to be just walking by when he saw an interesting story and stopped to record it. (So nimble was Liebling that many readers probably had no idea how heavy a man he was.) And what he recorded remains the best literature on boxing yet written.

Liebling's focus on the physical aspects of a bout could, at times, take on the properties of film. In a 1959 piece, "An Artist Seeks Himself," Liebling is sitting ringside at a match between Floyd Patterson and Brian London. The fight is meant as a warm-up for Patterson's title bout with Ingemar Johansson. London is seen as no serious threat, and though he hangs on longer than expected, the big Brit eventually goes down. Liebling gives us a wonderful view of this beating. Patterson hit London hard in each rib cage, so hard that London's ribs "began to glow red through the skin." A right to the jaw summons a look of surprise from London's face, like a man who "finds the water nearly ice." Patterson then tore into his foe with savage body shots that left London beaten and defenseless. After the fifth round, London could not punch with any authority: "The snap was out of his arms." Yet London kept coming. He was knocked to one knee at the end of the tenth, but he came out for the eleventh. Patterson, "with a flurry of blows, drove him across the ring toward where [Liebling] sat." A final punch and that was it. London hit the canvas, first with his left hip, then his shoulder. The force of the fall knocked the wind out of him. He was through. "He lay with his left cheek against the canvas," floored by a Patterson left.

Liebling's refined treatment of "the sweet science," as he called boxing, was enhanced when he met up with Cassius Clay in early 1962. In "Poet and Pedagogue," Liebling spends time with the Olympic champion as he readies for his New

York City pro debut against a hard-hitting, "hungry" fighter, Sonny Banks. When Liebling saw Clay win the gold medal in Rome in 1960, he noted that the young fighter "had a skittering style, like a pebble scaled over water. He was good to watch, but he seemed to make only glancing contact." Liebling is impressed by Clay's skills, especially his speed, but thinks he may not hold up in longer bouts. This assessment would change. Liebling also connects Clay's poetic demeanor to his fluid motion inside the ring. The young heavyweight is cocky but smooth, a combination that amuses the writer. (When Clay recites a poem about Floyd Patterson while doing sit-ups, Liebling notes that Clay is perhaps the sole American poet who could recite in such a manner. Not even T.S. Eliot could do it.) But when he describes the fight itself, Liebling's appreciation of Clay deepens. Banks knocks Clay down, the first time Clay met the canvas since his amateur days. He is up at the count of two and remains, in Liebling's words, "cool." Clay got right back up, maintained his steady mode of attack, cuffing, jabbing, slapping, sticking, "the busy hands stinging like bees."

Here we see the first comparison of Clay's fists to stinging bees—a comparison that, with his butterfly float, would soon help define the Ali legend. Liebling finds the comparison so apt that he varies it slightly when describing Clay's incessant jabs to Banks that flatten his nose across his face. Banks had difficulty breathing, Clay's "intellectual pace" too swift for him to match. He kept going with the left hook, "but he was like a man trying to fight off wasps with a shovel." Clay wins the bout in four, and Liebling knows that the kid has a bright future. Thirteen months later, writer and poet hook up again as Clay prepares to fight Doug Jones, a better fighter than Banks but to Clay a slight detour on his way to Sonny Liston and the title. However, the bout goes ten rounds and is close throughout, and there are moments when Clay "showed signs of severe apprehension," even though he receives a unanimous decision.

But it is the Madison Square Garden crowd's reaction to Clay that Liebling finds intriguing—and disturbing. Clay's national profile had risen in the year since Liebling last wrote of him, and with it came the tremendous scorn of those who hated his cockiness and his poetry. As Liebling put it, the crowd saw the fight as "a vast allegorical struggle between the Modest Underdog and Mr. Swellhead Bigmouth Poet." After Clay was handed the judges' decision, the crowd's "anti-intellectualism truly raised its ugly head and its still uglier voice." Liebling doesn't dwell on this, but it weighs on his thoughts. Had he lived to see Clay become champion, change his name to Ali, and then refuse to fight in Vietnam, there would have been more than just crowd noise to deplore. Liebling's essays on these events would have been fascinating to read. But he died not long after the above bout, before the full flowering of the man he considered poetry in gloves. Liebling understood Clay from the start, one artist tipping his hat to another. His death not only robbed boxing of its man of letters, it cut short a relationship just taking root.

Liebling's career spanned a period when sportswriting was considered by many a literary pursuit. Writers like Red Smith, Jimmy Cannon, and Jim Murray poured over their words as seriously as any author, and for them there were no stray lines or tossed-off observations that couldn't be tightened and polished. Smith and Cannon were fine stylists with an ear for clubhouse slang. Murray was a bit more playful, though at times his humor could cut through the self-regard of sports officials. Perhaps his most famous line came in a critique of the Indianapolis 500. Murray suggested a new command to begin the race: "Gentlemen, start your coffins." Race officials found this tasteless, but Murray could care less. "People need to be amused, shocked, titillated or angered," he said in his autobiography. "But if you can amuse or shock or make them indignant enough, you can slip lots of information into your message."

Among those bearing messages today, only a handful prod superstar athletes, team owners, or complacent fans with any regularity. Part of this is because those who are ambitious don't bother with a dead form like print. They look to get into sports broadcasting, where the real action is, and once there even fewer desire a conflict with the status quo. For one thing, broadcasters are by and large less contentious than those pounding keys to meet deadlines. You won't see many angry sports fanatics wearing network blazers and spitting their contempt at network cameras. Sports broadcasting is showbiz; broadcasters must keep to the script ("You're looking *live* at a jam-packed and festive Mile High Stadium") and make their observations as nonthreatening as possible without losing "credibility," or worse, ratings points.

This is not to say that "unpredictable" commentary by sports announcers is entirely verboten. Bill Walton made his mark as a "straightshooting" NBA analyst for NBC. The

UCLA legend and Trailblazer great, who overcame a stuttering problem to find his acid tongue, is never afraid to criticize or condemn player behavior, coaches' decisions or referees' calls, and this makes him a bit of a maverick to those professional fans who take a milder view of sports. Like Hubie Brown and Doug Collins, two former players and coaches who excel as hoops analysts, Walton is knowledgeable about the game. But his apparent need to appear "edgy" tends to undermine his analysis and reduces it to schtick.

There have been sports broadcasters for whom a low-profile worked beautifully. Curt Gowdy's distinctive voice was heard throughout the 1960s and '70s, calling football, baseball, college basketball games, and, as host of ABC's "The American Sportsman," fishing and hunting. If Gowdy offered contentious opinions about the sports he covered, they were smoothed over by his amiable baritone and enthusiasm for the games. Gowdy was knowledgeable and illuminative but casual, as though he were discussing the finer points of mending a chair. When he lit up to describe an exciting play, he did so effortlessly and within a breath was back to his original tone.

Like Gowdy, Vin Scully conveyed a sense of ease while describing his game, baseball, and his team, the Los Angeles Dodgers. Scully's voice was mellifluous in a nasal kind of way and he always sounded faintly congested. But it was a voice that enriched his play-by-play, and he never rushed it nor used it to fill dead air. Indeed, the sounds of the ballpark complemented Scully's style of announcing well. Even when calling notable plays, like the final pitch of a Sandy Koufax perfect game ("Two-and-two on Harvey Kuenn . . . one strike away . . ."), Scully harnessed the moment and made it conform to his pace, one that moved freely from inning to inning but never jumped ahead of the game itself. The kind of professional ease which defined Scully's and Gowdy's work is rarely seen today, although Al Michaels can pull it off, despite his role as Monday night ringmaster. Michaels is especially good when calling baseball, but until his network, ABC, decides once again to broadcast major league games, poor Al is stuck following the inflated Chris Berman and Hank Williams, Jr., demanding to know if we are "ready for some football."

If the number of refined broadcasters is small, then the number of contentious broadcasters verges on a percentage point. Some take "contentious" to mean anyone who raises his or her voice while calling a game or narrating highlights. Were this the case, contention would be omnipresent. But one need not shout to challenge the pieties and received wisdom of the major sports establishment. If one is intelligent and has access to a network audience (no easy combination), there are opportunities to say what most sportscasters either ignore or lack the will to say themselves.

Howard Cossell was an interesting case in this respect. His melodic if sometimes irritating voice was instantly recognizable, and his vocabulary set him apart from his peers. He could be entertaining and insightful but was always close to becoming the type of caricature that he himself would blast in better years—and ultimately became as his influence waned. Cossell's support for Muhammad Ali's draft resistance was perhaps his defining principled stand. He not only felt that Ali was right, he assailed boxing and the greater culture for banning Ali from the ring. Of course, Cossell never stopped congratulating himself for taking this stand— he was Howard Cossell after all. But for a major media figure to side with someone so vilified at a time when there were no guarantees that Ali would come back was, and is, a rare thing. Ali certainly appreciated this and he rewarded Cossell by giving him and the audience great performances on "Wide World of Sports." (Who can forget Ali's ongoing threat to remove Cossell's hairpiece before the cameras, or his theatrical altercation with Joe Frazier that sent the ABC studio into chaos?) The two clearly shared mutual affection for one another, although Cossell never withheld his criticisms of Ali. When the Greatest was well past his prime but continued to fight, Cossell openly declared that Ali was being foolish and that he should retire. The plaintive tones heard in Cossell's voice as he witnessed Ali's beating at the hands of Larry Holmes said it all. He was both saddened and disgusted, and he apologized to the viewers that they had to watch such a pathetic ending to a brilliant career.

While not as flamboyant a character as Cossell, Bob Costas has more or less assumed the late broadcaster's place as a well-spoken, opinionated network figure. Costas cut his teeth by calling Spirits of St. Louis games in the late days of the ABA.* He was (and remains) a decent basketball an-

---

*He later admitted that he did a poor imitation of Marv Albert, including the signature "Yes!" after key buckets. Ironically enough, Costas was picked by NBC to replace Albert as its top NBA announcer after the randy private life of Marvelous became public. Costas had long abandoned his Albertisms, yet he remained loyal to his colleague and early influence and told viewers that he could never match Albert's style of broadcasting.

nouncer, but his real talent emerged when working the base-ball beat. Costas's knowledge of the game is impressive; he matches stats to players with relative ease while bringing color to specific at-bats, pitcher-runner duels, managerial strategies, and the like. And though he is a veritable trove of information and anecdotes, Costas never gets in the way of a game nor allows himself to disrupt its flow. He respects baseball too much to overexplain a wild pitch, a bobbled grounder to short. But if sufficiently irked, Costas will not hold his tongue. His criticisms of the way baseball has been altered and promoted for the sake of grabbing a larger audi-ence can be withering and precise. Unlike many announcers (especially those on ESPN, where Costas sometimes appears), Costas has never warmed to the wild-card system nor to in-terleague play. He's not against change, he insists to those who see him as a stern traditionalist. He simply feels that the changes made were not in the best interests of the game. So strong are his beliefs that Costas was thought by some to be commissioner material. Costas himself blew this off, perhaps because it would take him away from what he loves most—calling games. It's an inspired idea, however unrealistic. Be-sides, if baseball truly wanted an activist commissioner who appreciated the very roots of the sport, it wouldn't have settled for Bud Selig, the owners' choice.

Cossell and Costas, as eloquent and cutting as they could be, were nevertheless hemmed in by television's strict bound-aries. Neither could—whether they wanted to or not—make the same critiques that one can make in print. At bottom, TV sports are entertainment; too much carping spoils the fun. So it is left to those who write to offset this cultural deficiency, and though many chose not to, there are two columnists who need little encouragement to step up and state their views.

Robert Lipsyte of *The New York Times* is one of the few remaining unabashed left-liberals working in the field today.* More amazing still, he doesn't run from the label. In fact, his politics have led him to both mourn and say good riddance to what he calls our dying sports culture. "Sports are over because they no longer have any moral resonance," he wrote in 1995. "They are merely entertainment, the bread and circuses of a New Rome." Lipsyte has no use for the guys who live for their games and who try to find meaning in staged rituals—regardless if they are average fans or his fellow sportswriters: "[T]he ultimate sissy is the male sports fan still hung on the romance of a SportsWorld that never quite existed, a psychic theme park of courage and tragedy and revenge and redemption that was rolled out every season by sissy sportswriters who were willing to be treated with contempt by athletes in return for a few minutes inside that male clubhouse." But, ultimately, we are all to blame because we the fans have helped to finance this degraded carnival to the tune of billions of dollars a year, and there's no end in sight. Says Lipsyte, "Instead of sports, we will happily root for human cartoons competing in athletic theme parks fueled

---

*While not primarily a sportswriter, Gerald Early has written about American sports from a left-academic perspective, and his essays on race, baseball, and boxing can be found in *The Culture of Bruising*. He also edited and penned the introduction to *The Muhammad Ali Reader*. Then there is Filip Bondy of the New York *Daily News*. An afficionado of soccer who considers (yet appreciates) the NFL as fascistic, Bondy is a liberal Creature and has written of the joys of watching Yankees games among the brutes in the Stadium's right-field bleachers.

without apology by violent thrills and endorsement dollars. We will buy team jerseys by color, not name. We will demand honest effort and drug-free play only because we need to feel that we can gamble with confidence." Lipsyte comes as close as he can to predicting a cultural downfall without resorting to a sandwich board and bullhorn.

Phil Mushnick of *The New York Post* and *TV Guide* has many of the same concerns as Lipsyte but lays them down in short, sharp bursts. He is Old Testament to Lipsyte's New. Mushnick rails against hypocrisy, commercialism, the promotion of violence as children's entertainment, sports journalists who sell out their reputations for a shot at TV stardom, and so on. Given the current landscape, Mushnick never runs out of topics. But what really motivates Mushnick is his personal sense of honor. The guy will not do the things he criticizes others for doing.* (For example, he refuses to appear on television.) This stance, of course, sets him up for reprisal; after all, Mushnick's newspaper is owned by Rupert Murdoch, whose political and financial dealings resemble Australian rules football played with hatchets. "Anybody preaching journalism within those pages is tainted," says Dick Schaap, host of ESPN's "The Sports Reporters" and a target of Mushnick's attacks. "As eloquent a statement as Mushnick can make on behalf of journalism, your statement

---

*Well, *almost* never. As do most moralists, Mushnick condemns hypocrisy while engaging in his own. When the Knicks traded for Latrell Sprewell, Mushnick denounced the team's owners for their win at any cost mentality. Sprewell, said Mushnick, was a thug and should not have been rewarded for his attack on his former coach, P. J. Carlisimo. Yet when Marv Albert, who pleaded guilty to assault, was hired to anchor Madison Square Garden Television's nightly wrap-up show "Sports Desk," Mushnick welcomed Albert back to the fold.

is diminished when you accept a check from Rupert Murdoch." But then, as Mushnick pointed out, Schaap works for Disney, a company whose hands are no less dirty than Murdoch's. Will Schaap quit *his* job? No, and neither will Mushnick, so long as he feels free to criticize Fox product in Murdoch's pages and raise the type of issues, like slave labor in Asian sweatshops, that his fellow Murdochians are too timid to address.

For all their moral outrage and devotion to untainted sports, neither Lipsyte nor Mushnick command much of a media following. They are not among those sports pundits who appear on every show that will have them, promoting yet another book about their glimpse inside the wild crazy world of this conference or that league. (Mitch Albom, a sportswriter for the *Detroit Free Press*, worked his way briefly outside of this circle with his 1998 bestseller, *Tuesdays with Morrie*, a book about friendship in the face of death.) Most of the guys who do this are regularly seen on "The Sports Reporters." Every Sunday morning Bill Conlin, John Feinstein, Tony Kornheiser, Michael Wilbon, Bob Ryan, and Mike Lupica sit with Dick Schaap and perform their version of "The McLaughlin Group." It's a semicomic give-and-take, the floor going to the loudest, brashest man there. And more often than not, that man is usually Mike Lupica.

A columnist for the New York *Daily News* and at one time *Esquire,* Lupica has made himself into one of the better-known and better-paid sportswriters in the country. But there is more to Lupica than sports media renown. For while his on-camera persona borders on sheer arrogance, his printed work is perhaps the most experimental one will find on any sports page in the country. Lupica's approach to sentence-making recalls the cut-up method championed by the late William S. Burroughs—random words set in a nonlinear sequence. This may help to explain his charm. His pieces in *Esquire*, while technically fine, betrayed a copy editor's polish not seen in the *Daily News*. The same is true of his current work in *ESPN Magazine*. Still, nothing Lupica writes is as extraordinary as his *Daily News* output. One may select at random any clipping and encounter English not heard or seen since Ed Wood convinced eccentric businessmen to finance his films. Indeed, Lupica shares with the infamous auteur a talent for creating odd, uncanny prose, and the similarities between them are striking.

Here is Lupica after Chicago won its sixth NBA crown: "There has never been much slapstick to the Chicago Bulls on the basketball court, even with Dennis Rodman on that court, looking like the Halloween Parade sometimes." Now here is Ed Wood, from his transvestite farce, *Glen or Glenda?*: "Modern man is a hardworking human. Throughout the day, his mind and his muscles are busy at building his modern world and its business administration . . . But life, even though its changes are slow, moves on." Note how the sly repetitions in each unfold to reveal strange but telling observations. Indeed, repetition defines much of Lupica's and Wood's work; and when employed judiciously, the results are often inspired. The day following Mark McGwire's 62nd homer, Lupica stated, "There are all the other records of American sports, and then there is that record. There are all the other games, despite what you have heard, and then there is this game." Wood serves up a similar helping in his sci-fi epic, *Plan 9 from Outer Space*. A wife tells her pilot-husband that she is not afraid of the aliens and ghouls running rampant. "The saucer's up *there*, and the cemetery's out *there*, but I'll be locked up in *there*," she says, nodding to their house. In this as in so much of his work, Wood anticipates Lupica and provides a blueprint for the latter's takes on sports.

Predictably, Lupica's inventive use of language did not make him a minor celebrity, but rather his personality. Such is the fate of the misunderstood artist. His attempts at TV humor, carried by a loud, whining delivery, were lowbrow but deemed commercial, and Lupica was awarded his own show on ESPN2. Despite the roars of his studio audience, Lupica's show faltered and back to his "Sports Reporters" seat he went. However, Lupica's effort was not unique: Other sports reporters have made moves to reach a wider audience. Keith Olbermann left Dan Patrick and ESPN to host what he thought would be an insightful "Big Show" on MSNBC. But instead of dealing with myriad issues, Olbermann quickly became ringmaster to the Monica Lewinsky circus and was so miserable that he ran off to Fox Sports and the comfort of familiar themes. Craig Kilborn, another ESPN grad, became host of Comedy Central's "The Daily Show," where he played the frat boy who said nasty things about everything and everyone (including the show's co-founder, who quit after suffering a number of sexually explicit insults). Kilborn's act amused the honchos at CBS who pegged him to replace that late, late-night fixture, Tom Snyder. No return to sports for Craig.

As professional sports fans seek greater celebrity, some showbiz celebrities reach for their dream—to be taken seriously as sports fanatics. Two personalities—one a TV actor, the other a feature film director—make much of their exalted fan status. Both have written books to show how closely they follow their favorite sports, and since they are celebrities their devotion is more profound than those who are not.

The TV actor, George Will, plays the nebbish scold on ABC's "This Week," a variety show that features current events. Will takes his onscreen character very seriously. He's the stern "moralist" who loves authority, who enjoys dining with the powerful, and who freely uses his copy of *Bartlett's Quotations* to show what a smart boy he is. It's a fine act and Will has done well with the character he's developed. But like most entertainers, Will looks to stretch and go against type. Since he is frail and probably unable to throw a ball (Nerf included) more than ten yards, it makes sense that he be a robust sports fanatic. Were he truly adventurous he would come out in favor of football, hockey or extreme fighting on pay-per-view. But Will knows that his fans don't want him to wander too far from his TV character, so he has settled on the traditionalist's game, baseball.

Will has written two books about the national pastime: *Men at Work* and *Bunts*. They are the kind of volumes seen on middle American bookshelves, pressed against first-editions of *Iacocca*, Stephen Ambrose's D-Day works, and perhaps Paul Reiser's meditations on the Dad thing. Like his political prose, Will's baseball writing is hard on the eye. He affects a "classical" style of sentence-building but has trouble establishing, and maintaining, a fluid rhythm. He is also fond of clichés. But his real weakness is listing statistics. Lots and lots of statistics—batting averages, ERAs, strikeouts per inning, percentages of screwballs hit for triples, and so on. By doing this Will tells the reader that he's done his homework, true to his character both onscreen and off. But as most sports fans know, popping off stats is simple. All one needs is a sports almanac or some other kind of record book, a decent memory and the willingness to employ numbers in an argument. Instant expertise. When Will gets away from the statistical ruse, he runs into analysis. At certain moments, he's not bad; occasional patches of interest crop up. But in the main he's tough to take.

One of Will's chief tactics is to take a hardened, "realist" position when discussing the game. There is much of this in *Men At Work* (the title itself implies a no-nonsense approach). Will dismisses those who see baseball in a pastoral light as "silly and sentimental" and otherwise romantic. To Will, the national pastime "involves blazing speeds and fractions of seconds . . . [t]he pace of the action is relentless." It is in assessments like this where Will tries to distance himself from his political work. There he is often quite silly about the role people should play as citizens (pull your levers and stay out of the way), and he is incredibly sentimental in the face of power (his glasses were fogged with mist during much of the Reagan era). But every so often his political tone seeps into his baseball work. Toward the end of *Men At Work*, Will states primly, "A baseball game is an orderly experience—perhaps too orderly for the episodic mentalities of television babies. A baseball game is, like a sentence, a linear sequence; like a paragraph, it proceeds sequentially. But to enjoy it you have to be able to read it. Baseball requires baseball literacy." *That's* the Georgie we know from *This Week*.

For all of his character's pretense, there are times when Will's writing brings joy to the reader. In *Bunts*, Will reprints several of his early baseball essays to give us a fuller picture of his fandom (and thus his expertise). In a piece from March 1974, he speaks of the turmoil he suffered as a young Cubs fan: "Spring, Earth's renewal, a season of hope for the rest of mankind, became for me an experience comparable to being slapped around the mouth with a damp carp. Summer was like being bashed across the bridge of the nose with a crowbar—ninety times. My youth was like one long rainy Monday in Bayonne, New Jersey."

This seasonal punishment may explain why as an adult Will supports the killing of strangers in distant lands: The young masochist turned sadist and pines to swing the crowbar himself. Then again this was early in his character's development, so he may have been experimenting with tone, trying on different masks. Whatever the case, the sight of boy George getting soaked in Bayonne is a pleasant one, as is the sound of that damp carp hitting his pursed mouth. Would that Sam Donaldson had been savvy enough to keep a few fish in his pocket for when Will got out of line. "Yeah, I got your bombing of Iraq right here, George . . ." SMACK!

Will is certainly maddening, but he is nowhere near Spike Lee, perhaps the most obnoxious basketball fan ever seen in Madison Square Garden. Lee's relation to hoops is puzzling. On the one hand, he wrote and directed *He Got Game*, which has as its opening credit sequence a heartfelt tribute to the beauty of basketball as has ever been staged for film. Though it resembles a Nike spot, the sequence neverthe- less shows us how the game cuts across class and racial lines as boys and girls, young men and young women, play on dirt and on blacktop, on farms, and on urban streets. The music of Aaron Copland gives the sequence a fine American texture that heightens the feeling but does not cheapen the sentiment. The film itself cannot compete with the opening, but there are nice moments that follow—especially when Denzel Washington tells Ray Allen the story of Earl Monroe, "Black Jesus," as shots of the legend performing his magic for the Baltimore Bullets pop in and out of the scene.

In *He Got Game*, Lee employed his considerable film tal- ents to illustrate the greatness of his favorite sport. What to make then of his book, *Best Seat in the House*, a semiautobio- graphical account of Lee's lifelong crush on the New York Knicks and how the team's fortunes paralleled his own growth as a filmmaker. The parallels are awkwardly constructed, but that's the least of *Best Seat*'s problems. His collaboration with friend Ralph Wiley resulted in a poorly-written, reckless book that few white writers would get away with, primarily in those sections that deal with race.

In fact, *Best Seat* is filled with racial huckstering. When assessing the history of sports on film, Lee leaves no cracker uncrumbled as he brushes aside sense and facts. He recalls watching the original *Rocky* in a theater and is appalled as the white people around him cheer Rock's victory over the "uppity, loudmouthed, flamboyant nigger," Apollo Creed. The only thing is, Creed wins that bout, not Rocky. Stallone's character does give the fictional heavyweight champ a fright, but he falls short on points and neither is in the mood for a rematch. (After the film won an Academy Award, the mood changed.) That Creed is a Muhammad Ali type who looks to massacre a club fighter for publicity and is nearly beaten for his arrogance (and that Ali himself pulled similiar stunts late in his career) somehow strikes Lee as an incitement to a lynching. If anything Creed is more blaxploitation thug than D. W. Griffith blackface—not the most uplifting of portrayals, but then all the main characters in *Rocky* are equally cartoonish. No matter. Lee eventually settled the score in *Do the Right Thing* by having Sal's pizzeria burned to the ground by a rightcous black mob. How many of the white mutha-fuckas cheered *that*?

Lee feels the same way about *Hoosiers*. To him it was racist propaganda set in a time "when 'nigras knew' their place." As he later told *The Village Voice*, *Hoosiers* was a "glorious return to the days when teams were teams and there was no such thing as the fast break, when we didn't have all this fancy nigger shit with behind-the-back-passes and jams, when basketball was 'pure.' " Lee must know that in the early fifties a small school of white boys did indeed capture the Indiana state basketball crown. If one made a film about this, how else could it be portrayed?* Unlike some of Lee's efforts, there are no supremacist speeches in *Hoosiers*. Gene Hackman does not get up before his team and say, "Boys, I want you to play 'pure' basketball, none of that fancy nigger shit. You hear me?" He does stress team play and the value of creating passing lanes. After all, he has only seven players on his squad and is forced to adopt a conservative strategy. Had he a young Bob Cousy or "Jumpin' " Joe Fulks, both of whom opened up the game in those early years with "behind-the-back-passes" and quick shooting off the fast break, perhaps Hackman's team would have been less "offensive" to Lee. But then, given Lee's temperament, perhaps not.

Lee's race baiting is not confined to the cinema. He tells how he was criticized for his comments about Larry Bird in *She's Gotta Have It*. His character, Mars Blackmon, says that Bird is not only ugly, he is overrated as a player. Lee defends this not by saying simply, "That's my opinion"—far too pedestrian a line—but by cloaking his comments in the red,

*One *can* say that while historically true (to the degree that any film treatment of real events can be completely accurate: See *Malcolm X*), the plot of *Hoosiers* does set up as its climax the victory of white farm boys over a team that has black city kids. Does this in itself constitute racism? Lee believes so, and no doubt many white tribalists were happy with the result. But to end the film any other way would constitute revisionism at its most absurd, so the only alternative would have been not to make *Hoosiers* at all. Lee doesn't say this. Does he think it?

black, and green. "Black people were tired of hearing how Larry Bird was the greatest basketball player ever. Bird this, Bird that . . . Mars was articulating a frustration about the accomplishments of black folks, how they are denied their due all over." While Lee grudgingly admits that Bird was indeed "a great player," he revises history to make it seem that the NBA was involved in a White Hope conspiracy. What other white player in the mid-eighties received the same praise as Bird? Kevin McHale, an intregal part of those Celtics championship teams, certainly did not. And what of Magic, Kareem, Dr. J, Isiah, Drexler, Barkley, and Hakeem? Their due was denied? Unable to make a cogent political or social point (did Lee mean to suggest that ordinary "black folks" were eclipsed by Bird's celebrity? If so, what of ordinary white, brown, and yellow folks?), Lee cups his hands and yells, "Racist," his magic word when pressed for an argument.

Yet Lee has a double standard when it comes to racism. In Barcelona for the 1992 summer games to watch his Dream Team pals taunt the less fortunate, Lee quotes Charles Barkley laughing off his flagrant foul against an Angolan player by saying, "Well, he might have pulled a spear on me." At first Lee's antennae senses danger, but then he admits that "maybe I was not giving Charles enough credit for his satirical slant . . . I laughed when I heard it, so maybe Charles knows what he's doing." Sure. Imagine if Larry Bird had deliberately elbowed an African player and then used the spear-chucker line to excuse it. Satire? Hardly. That overrated ugly cracker would have had a Klansman's hood slipped onto his head by Lee, who would then berate the racist media for making Bird a hero to white kids—the same kids who sit at home and watch *Hoosiers!*

When not playing the race game, Lee plays up his importance to the Knicks. From his courtside seat in the Garden, Lee watches every movement on the floor and reacts accordingly. During a Knicks–Bulls game, Scottie Pippen dunks on Patrick Ewing, knocks the big man down, and then momentarily straddles him. Lee boasts to his readers, "I would be kicking my way up, if it was me down there. Don't be dangling your gonies over me, you mother . . ." But instead, Lee jumps up and screams to referee Jake O'Donnell: "He's taunting him, Jake! You can't allow that! Tech, tech!" Pippen strolls by Lee's seat and says, "Sit the fuck down, Spike," which, if Lee had a sense of humor about himself, would have been the title of his book. But Lee is a full-blown megalomaniac; he truly believes he is equal to the refs, the coaches, and most of the players in the league, in stature and in celebrity. *Sit the fuck down?*

At his dizziest, Lee acts as if he were the Knicks' head coach—or at least a top assistant. In describing his battle with the Pacers' Reggie Miller during Game 1 of the 1994 Eastern Conference finals, when Miller lit up for 25 points during the fourth quarter, Lee justifies his jumping and screaming on the sideline by saying that the Knicks are "his" team and that they needed his boost. He quotes Marv Albert chastising his behavior on national television, but quickly dismisses the critique.* Lee paid "500 bananas a pop" for the right to act like a fool, and besides, Miller is also to blame for making him "part of it." Lee ultimately defends his actions in the Knicks–Pacers game by saying that other fans and the newspapers unfairly blamed *him* for the loss. He claims he was "figuratively mugged." When he goes to Indianapolis for Game 6, he complains of the media crush there. "I never heard about Jack Nicholson going through anything like this." (Well, Nicholson doesn't jump up and down and scream at opposing players.) The *Indianapolis News,* anticipating Lee's arrival, provides Pacers fans with a cut-out mask of the director's face to wear during the game. Naturally, Lee compares this to Klan tactics. After the Knicks win and send the series back to New York for Game 7, Lee says he and a friend must run for their lives lest they are strung up by crazed Hoosiers.

Once the tirades die down, Lee becomes introspective. "You look at things through your own eyes," he candidly admits. "Most of us don't have the gift of being in someone else's shoes, looking at other people's lives from their perspective, to see why they see things the way *they* do, and maybe that's unfortunate. Maybe I do identify with pesky point guards playing the passing lanes, snatching the ball from the big men's hands, dodging elbows. Those guys are more like me. I hope I'm not limited to seeing the Game from that one point of view."

As long as he has season tickets and some measure of

---

*This before the revelations of Albert's private affairs. If only Spike knew . . .

celebrity, Spike Lee need never worry about seeing the Game from one point of view. He'll see it from the coaches, refs, and players point of view as well and will inform them of the fact. He got game, all right. Just pity those who pay to sit right behind him.

4

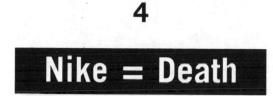
Nike = Death

We will mature in tandem with the inexorable penetration
of sports into the global psyche.

—FROM NIKE'S 1997 ANNUAL REPORT

The brand is sacred.

—PHILIP H. KNIGHT, NIKE CHAIRMAN

Sports marketing, known to insiders as "the Monkey Thrust,"* has rendered archaic all other methods of propaganda. Compared to political ads, the M. Thrust is an alien scroll that defies human translation. Set against standard consumer spots, the M. Thrust moves at carnivore speed. Curious thing, the Thrust. Those whose minds have felt its sting swear by little else, and if pushed, will fight to protect the honor of something they themselves can never really define.

Monkey Thrusting, ever sublime, is but one gesture made in our corporate world. The purpose of marketing is to get a company's product or logo crammed down the throats of

*Where this term originated is anyone's guess. One theory holds that Rosser Reeves, master of 1950s advertising, coined the phrase after watching a caged monkey reach for a TV just beyond the bars, becoming increasingly irate with each failed thrust. This amused Reeves no end, and he reportedly began to use caged monkeys as focus groups for new commercials. The ads that drove the apes insane had "that Monkey Thrust," and so, it was hoped, would have a similiar effect on consumers.

consumers. This effort assumes many forms. Sometimes it is done bluntly and obviously, like force-feeding a goose to make *foi gras*. Other times a subtler approach is used. Take "virtual signage," an upscale method of computerized tagging. As you watch, say, a baseball game, and you get the center-field shot of pitcher vs. batter, there on the wall behind home plate is an ad for a sports merchandising company. Or so it seems. Thanks to the fine folk at Princeton Video Image, the "ad" is electronically placed against the wall; it does not physically exist in the ballpark itself (fans there have other visual delights to engage them). Thus blank space is put to good use, ad revenues increase, and the home viewer need not wait until commercial time to receive his or her product "placement" amid the comforts of home.

"Virtual signage" is a step above conventional ballpark ads. For decades signs touting tobacco and beer lined every outfield, and slogans served as targets for the game's power hitters. While the signs still exist (and have diversified to include banks and bottled water), they lack the fluency of the new virtual brands. As is usually the case, those who profit from a marketing strategy speak as if the public stand to gain as well. Sam McCleery, vice president of sales and marketing at Princeton Video Image, told *The New York Post* that virtual signage puts more money into team and network pockets "without further cluttering the field or adding between inning commercials"—which, according to McCleery, should be eliminated to quicken the game . . . and of course allow his company "virtual" access to more advertising space.

It is, perhaps, fanciful to think that between inning commercials will be quietly erased. Indeed, *any* empty space makes a hustler's mouth wet, so why trade one form of marketing for another? Why not seize both? The more products the better; and if dame luck is truly with us, we'll soon see holographic ads floating above diamonds nationwide. Bright, ethereal figures owned by Disney or Warner Bros. frolic in midair as a closer tries to keep the tying run on first while pitching to the batter low and away. But the tension of the moment is broken by holo-Simba or cyber-Bugs prancing at bleacher level, capturing the attention of kids, stirring the ire of drunks who throw beer bottles through images that aren't really there.

For the time being, however, we must subsist on traditional brand placement, either in commercials, logos in hockey rinks or beneath the scorer's table at NBA games (which change every minute from GATORADE to NIKE to NBA. COM, a pure commodity flux). And let's not overlook corporate "sponsorship," i.e., the paid hijacking of college football bowl games. At one time the best teams in the country would clash at the beginning of the year in various bowl games— Cotton, Sugar, Orange, Rose. Gradually the number of bowls increased, from Bluebonnet to Gator to Fiesta to (son of Orange?) Citrus. Before long, alumni boosters and their corporate pals figured, *Hell! Let's go whole fuckin' hog!* Eyes wide, lips moist, they created all manner of bowls, the design of which was of secondary concern. The *point,* of course, was to grab every available buck, so ultimately it didn't matter if the teams playing were any good: Let the slobs at home worry about a match between two 7–4 squads; if one of them is Notre Dame, well, at least marquee value is slightly enhanced. Remember the Gip, and all that jazz.

As the bowl universe expanded, names became a problem. There simply weren't enough colorful names for each game. A solution was soon reached: Why not name the new bowl games after the corporate sponsors themselves (while adding sponsor names to the established bowls)? Like golf and tennis tournaments before it, a company's logo would be in shot for most of the game, both on the field itself and with the network graphics when the score is shown before and after commercial breaks. Add to this the announcers mentioning the company again and again over a two-hour period, and brother, you're in revenue heaven.* Occasional slips are inevitable, "Third-and-six for Tennessee at the Tostitos thirty-four-yard line . . ."† But in America, excessive plugging is expected. Besides, once you reach the point where a bowl game serves only to promote an on-line service, words like *excessive* are meaningless.

Bowl games are the least of it. Stadiums and arenas are now corporate emblems and games played within them are part of the promotional effort. The RCA Dome, 3-Com Park,

---

*And then there's the "sponsoring" of stats, a digit-shaped stage where the likes of NASDAQ, Miller Lite, and McDonald's present, in full-costume, the number of fumbles, rebounds, or strikeouts in each respective game. Minutiae made simple for the common fan—and now this . . .

†After Kansas State beat Nebraska in November 1998, Wildcats fans, hoping their team would be chosen to play in the Fiesta Bowl for the national championship, actually tossed tortilla chips onto the field as a way of expressing their desire to Tostitos, the Bowl's corporate sponsor. However, after losing to Texas A&M, Kansas State had to settle for the Alamo Bowl, where rental cars, not chips, gave the game its luster.

Tropicana Field, Fleet Center, United Center, MCI Center, Continental Arena, America West Arena, among many to be named later (what fresh titles await the replacements for Tiger Stadium, Wrigley Field, and Fenway Park?), stand as monuments to faceless CEOs and their partners. It almost makes one cling to Coors Field, despite its connection to a family of neo-fascist Clampetts. Although Rockies home games help to remind beer drinkers of the smooth taste of Coors, there remains a hint of the old order when the egos of Comiskey and Ebbets overshadowed the need to push product. Not the best situation, but certainly preferable to, and in a perverse way more personal than the present corporate arrangement where "public" space serves private concerns.

But stadiums are static things and have limited promotional reach. Team symbols, however, penetrate every layer of American life and remind us that from the market there is no escape. No matter where one travels the sight is inevitable: youths wearing at various angles the "official" caps of the Raiders, Yankees, Bulls, Packers, and Cowboys, as well as complementing jackets and jerseys, PROPERTY OF T-shirts, and the like. On urban streets, county roads and suburban cul-de-sacs, American teens and young adults serve as human billboards for the NFL, NBA, NHL, and MLB. They do so voluntarily, eagerly, and their taste in uniforms and symbols transcends personal appearance. It now alters the way teams develop their color schemes, logos, and overall design. As with so much else in our bright culture, focus groups determine which way a sports apparel designer will go: widen the pinstripes, lose the cheetah's grin, add a green zig, a blue zag, and so on. Since teens themselves are the target market for uniform knockoffs, it follows that they should have some say in the design. This, of course, has led to some truly horrific results, and it takes an aesthetically detached or extremely well-paid athlete to have the nerve to don such things.

Take the Toronto Raptors uniform, easily the *worst* design job in the history of pro basketball. Made commercial by *Jurassic Park,* raptors were seen as strong, quick, agile, and aggressive—a perfect team symbol with market appeal. Since subtlety is for losers, the Toronto franchise went with what was a clear focus group favorite: a growling cartoon raptor wearing a Raptors uniform and holding a basketball. The rest of the jersey conformed to the prehistoric premise, complete with "Flintstones" lettering and streaks randomly placed. In short, one ugly fucker. But the designers at SME, the company responsible for the look, knew that beauty is pocket-deep. Before the Raptors took to the floor in their first NBA season, the team's jersey and related merchandise sold remarkably well, raising millions of dollars in sales as well as the profile of the franchise. Not bad for a team that became a way station for wealthy free agents en route to other cities.

Ultimately, most kids attracted to sports are attracted to the personalities who wear the designs. This attraction is of course catered to by the sports apparel companies, and so kids (and, sadly, some adults) walk around with other people's names on their backs. In no other area of celebrity culture is one encouraged to assume, as it were, the identity of the star one admires. And it's simple too. Just buy the jersey with the appropriate number and presto! You are Michael Jordan (#23, though connoisseurs also own #45, which he wore briefly upon his return to the game from baseball), Grant Hill (#33), Brett Favre (#4), Shaquille O'Neal (#32 in Magic white, #34 in Laker gold), Allen Iverson (#3), Troy Aikman and Kobe Bryant (both #8), Chris Webber (whose #4 has followed him from Michigan to Golden State to Washington to Sacramento to . . .), Deion Sanders (#21), and even Dennis Rodman (#91 in Bulls red, #73 in Lakers gold). While no sane person believes they "are" the athlete whose number and name they display, there is a surrender of self that's hard to ignore. But then celebrity jocks lead much richer lives than the peasants who revere them. Some illusion is expected.

The illusion, however, has two sides. As the thousands of Jordans and Hills stroll about, highlight reels in their heads, the real deals are busy being "branded"—a sly marketing strategy that reduces celebrity jocks to their essence, namely, product. Like the items they endorse, star athletes are brands with specific labels attached. But the labeling process is not an easy one, and much money is spent to find the right combination of ingredients that will ensure consumer loyalty or at least spark consumer interest. Once an athlete/ brand is established, it is unleashed to hawk everything from soda pop to chips to buckets of fries. It smiles, it laughs, it wishes to improve our lives. It seems almost human, yet if it were it would not be a brand name pitching other brands. It shed its mortal skin to reveal the commodity within.

This is pretty much the way agents and Monkey Thrust-ers view the athletes given them to sell: prime cuts served to the discerning consumer. (A DirecTV ad campaign literally showed NFL stars like Brett Favre, John Elway, and Jerry Rice as supermarket items wheeled about by shoppers.) Shaquille O'Neal has been through this process since his NBA arrival in 1992. Shaq was "the first pro sports star to be packaged from the start more as an entertainment brand than an athlete," wrote Jeff Jensen in *Advertising Age*. The Shaq Pack included endorsements for Reebok and Pepsi, a career in hip-hop, and a shot at movie stardom. Shaq was also to play basketball for the Orlando Magic, though at the time this seemed an afterthought, something to keep the big man busy between commercial gigs.* He had, it was hoped, the same market appeal of one Michael Jordan, whose smile alone shattered demographics and made moot the term "crossover." Brand Shaq would expand the horizon set by Jordan where money rained and profits grew.

While his early Pepsi spots received praise from those who praise such things (writers on the ad beat, "Entertainment Tonight" anchors), Shaq's overall media effect was as flat as his foul shooting in crunch time. His hip-hop sound was trite and tame, perhaps because he failed to go for the throat. Had Shaq gone full gangsta, a forty-sippin' blunt-smokin' bitch-slappin' thug with his AK and fuck-you stare, he might have blasted through the Will Smith wall into

---

*This led to some criticism from the other basketball Magic, Earvin Johnson, who suggested that Shaq develop his game rather than a rap persona. Johnson himself waited until retirement before he became a bad talk show host, a move that would have been compromised if made during his championship runs.

something no other pro athlete would dare attempt. God knows white teens would have creamed in their baggy Lees and CD sales would have shot up. But Shaq wanted more than rap notoriety. He dreamed of big screen success, and who would cast a seven-foot-one drive-by shooter as a lovable genie or a crime-fighting metal man? No, safe mindless beats were best for Shaq's rap side. Hollywood may like crazy Negroes, but not when they're the length of most story conference tables.

The one marketing area where Brand Shaq was expected to excel was moving Reebok sneakers. When he first signed with Reebok for five years at $3 million per, it was thought that Nike's Air Jordans were doomed. "Shaq is next," said Reebok chairman Paul Fireman. "We will use Shaq to catapult to leadership throughout the world." The company designed a signature sneaker, the Shaq Attaq, attached the big man's image to their company logo, then leaned back and waited for the windfall. But the world withstood Reebok's Attaq, and Air Jordan flew by unhindered. Even Shaq's move from Orlando to L.A., where it was assumed that his career would *really* take off, did nothing to raise the profile or enhance the market value of his sneaker. After losing $3.4 million in its first quarter of 1998, Reebok cut Shaq loose, the legacy of his Attaq left to the mercy of future shoe historians.

Before this rather sad ending, Reebok made attempts to turn their fortunes around. The company designed a newer version of Shaq's sneaker and licensed Warner Bros. Consumer Products "to sell a low-price line of WB Sport/Shaq branded footwear through mass merchants," according to *Ad-*

vertising Age. This strategy was part of the larger "repositioning" of Brand Shaq undertaken by Management Plus, the big Brand's sports marketing agency. *Repositioning* is M. Thrustspeak for structure overhaul, streamlining a failing model. "Now we're creating an evolved vision that will capture the imagination of our partners," boasted Leonard Armato, president of Management Plus. But the vision blurred and Shaq failed to make the transition necessary to keep Reebok happy. The two parted ways while Shaq's handlers sought to create a line of footwear and sports apparel that extended their client's persona, otherwise known as "relaunching."

To be fair, Shaq's endorsement slide paralleled that of other big-name players: Larry Johnson and Converse; Grant Hill and Fila; Allen Iverson, Glenn Robinson, Emmitt Smith, Larry Walker and Reebok. For some strange reason, young fans didn't respond to the lure of their heroes. Clearly something was amiss. But then came Kobe Bryant, an *actual* teenager playing in the NBA; not so much a role model as a fantasy peer. Although the number of NBA teens is rising, Kobe has so far been the best. And that he came out of high school swaddled in Laker gold and was placed alongside Shaq made marketers' tongues hang near their feet. Like seasoned pimps in port, they set upon the kid, doubtless convinced that young Kobe's hide would bring in major bucks for years to come. But first they had to make the kid delectable, a "fresh" catch.

This took little work. It helped Kobe's handlers that their product was intelligent, especially for a jock. He spoke several languages, including Japanese, which made that overseas market a definite lock. (Plus, "Kobe" is a fine cut of Japanese steak which his father, Jelly Bean Bryant, fancied. Name and metaphor were ultimately joined.) He was well mannered and behaved off-court, which pleased David Stern. He was to be the first true Teen Brand, a boy in adult packaging. Everyone, it seemed, had his ear, including MJ himself who, during a televised Bulls/Lakers game, passed words of advice to his possible heir in full view of NBC's large NBA audience. Kobe listened, smiled, then was beaten off-dribble and scored upon by the crafty old Bull. Kobe returned the favor in bursts, but he had yet gained the ease with which the Master stunned his prey. Thus a superstar prepares.

Kobe signed endorsement deals with Spalding Sports Worldwide and Adidas America. Executives from both companies waxed rhapsodic when discussing Kobe's profit potential. "Kobe basically embodies what the NBA is about right now: youth, excitement, charisma, and charm," said Dan Touhey, Spalding's product manager of retail basketball. "He's showtime," added Sonny Vaccaro, director of sports promotions for Adidas. "Signing Kobe was a major step for Adidas, the boldest step it's ever taken in this new era of Adidas. If we've guessed wrong, then I don't know what's right." Spalding financed Kobe's signature basketball line aimed at an upscale hoops demographic; no mere playground ball, this. Adidas wanted Kobe's imprimatur on its entire product line. Compared to these deals, Nintendo's Kobe Bryant's NBA Courtside, a video game starring the Laker prince, was a quaint sidelight. One had to admire the TV ad that promoted it. A sportscaster gets so excited watching cartoon

Kobe spin and slam that he touches the real Kobe's hand. Suggestively. Our hero, however, recoils upon contact, proof that Kobe is many things—but a faggot? Ha!

If Kobe has any reservations about the way he is peddled, few have heard them. Why complain? Kobe certainly knows that he is in a sweet financial position; and barring a premature career-ending injury or some unforeseen illegal or criminal act (known as the "O.J. factor"), his brand value will increase with each profitable quarter. To the Kobe-wannabes watching, this is how nature intended it. After all, a lifetime of television absorption has conditioned them to accept that the personal is commercial; that one's ultimate expression lies in the quip that seals a thirty-second spot. This is why so many high school players spend their junior and senior years auditioning for pro scouts. They cannot wait for the moneyed life to begin, to reach that plateau where one's name is adorned with ®, or at the very least ™.

If basketball cornered the market of dreams, then golf remained a random thought—until Tiger. Before the amateur phenom turned pro, golf was something that suburban white guys watched on slow Sunday afternoons. It was a game defined by plaid pants, soft "oohhhs" from the gallery, mellow commentary by Pat Summerall and Chris Shenckel, and the only blacks seen were those toting the bags of their bosses. Yes, there was Lee Elder and Calvin Peete, driving and chipping their way up to par. But they and the handful of other black golfers posed no threat to the nine-iron white rule of the PGA Tour. Their position was analogous to the "leaders" of the South African black "homelands" that existed alongside the apartheid state. They played on the same courses with white golfers, even won a tournament or two; but it was clear who ran the show. Then the show underwent revisions.

By the time Tiger Woods entered the PGA stage, most of the older black golfers had retired or moved on to the senior circuit. As John Feinstein pointed out in his entertaining essay, "The First Coming, Tiger Woods: Master or Martyr?," the PGA suddenly became concerned that the true color of its sport was now too obvious for comfort. Or marketing. "We have a very serious problem," said Tim Finchem, commissioner of the PGA Tour in 1994. "Our tour looks nothing like our country looks." (Doubtless to many white golf fans listening, this was a reason *why* they loved the PGA Tour.) When Tiger Woods won the 1997 Masters going away, the PGA knew that its marketing problem was solved: Here in a single twenty-one-year-old was an MJ, a Shaq, a Kobe. Tiger lent the Tour NBA flash; he hit the ball with authority and finesse, his drives as beautiful as a Michael jumper. Add Tiger's endorsement deals with American Express and Nike and pro golf looked as if it had joined the late twentieth century.

Of course, a few old-timers chafed at the change. Not only did Tiger represent the darker breeds rising in stature and power, he also was part of a wave of young players who would in time smash their elders against the rocks. But it was Tiger's complexion that stirred resentment, primarily in Fuzzy Zoeller, the Tour's good ole boy and cracker barrel wit. Upon Tiger's win at Augusta, Zoeller, affecting a Junior Samples air, told a CNN camera crew, "The little boy's playing great out there. Just tell him not to serve fried chicken at the dinner next year. Or collard greens or whatever it is they serve." Zoeller's remarks led to outrage. He apologized twice, was pressured to pull out of one of his favorite tournaments, the Greater Greensboro Open, and was released from an endorsement deal with Kmart. In his essay, John Feinstein tried somewhat to set Zoeller's comments in context and employed the reliable "politically incorrect" to define the Fuzz man's humor.* But as matters stood, Zoeller may have well called Tiger a cannibal pygmy savage. The end result could not have been much worse.

Tiger eventually forgave Zoeller for his indiscretion and got on with the business of golf. As Feinstein revealed, Team Tiger, a subsidiary of the International Management Group, "the most powerful and omnipresent sports management company in the world," was primarily concerned with fattening its collective wallet, often at the expense of its client's game. Like Kobe, Tiger did not protest. He too embraced the NBA aesthetic: First, nail down the deals; once you are rich beyond care, you may then concentrate on polishing your natural skills. Then again, maybe not. As so many young athletes have shown, the race for endorsements never ends. Tiger was no different. He dutifully climbed over bundles of cash as he made his way to the green; and who's to say that as he lined up a putt, he didn't for a second think, *Damn! I*

---

*Feinstein even suggested, albeit obliquely, that the spirit of Freedom Summer dwelled somewhere within Fuzzy, obscured by the media circus his remarks had inspired. In other words, Fuzzy might *say* this shit, but underneath was a man who'd risk his life to register blacks to vote in segregationist Mississippi. Well, wouldn't we all?

wish I'd sold the rights to this shot! If Tiger ever has regrets like this, he has only to rub the Nike swoosh on his shirt or cap and solace will be restored.

Indeed, it was with Nike where Tiger found brand-name peace of mind (reportedly worth $40 million). And being the philanthropic company that it is, Nike wished to extend Tiger's peace to those impoverished souls that had never seen a golf course, much less a tournament, in their young lives. Thus the post-Masters ad blitz featuring a series of multicolored kids proclaiming, "I am Tiger Woods"—not "I like Tiger Woods" or "Tiger Woods is my hero" or "Tiger Woods: Whatta guy!" Too simple and sane an approach. Instead Nike suggested that America's youth indentify with Tiger as would someone suffering personality disorder: "But I told you, officer, *I am Tiger Woods!!*" An impressive riff on the youth habit of wearing a celeb jock's jersey. Since there is no true golf uniform, kids have only Tiger's flesh to grab on to. And thoughtfully placed between flesh and groping fingers is clothing provided by Nike.

There are many athletic apparel companies, Reebok, Adidas, Starter, and Converse among them. But none so far has equalled Nike's impact on American culture. The swoosh is omnipresent, its checkmark frame as familiar and comforting as the Stars and Stripes (all that is left is for Congress to pass a bill prohibiting the burning of Nike merchandise). So prevalent is the swoosh that one wonders why the Christian Right hasn't dubbed it the Sign of the Beast: Pat Roberston could make connections to old pagan symbols and pray for Divine vengeance while Gary Bauer sees homosexuals behind the proliferation of the design. It may yet happen. Until that time, however, we must assess the meaning of Nike without the guidance of His cultural warriors, too busy helping queers become breeders and kneelers before crosses.

The rise of Nike has been described in a number of books, most amusingly in *Where the Suckers Moon: An Advertising Story* by Randall Rothenberg. There also is a fine account in *Taking to the Air: The Rise of Michael Jordan* by Jim Naughton. In brief, Nike was co-founded by Bill Bowerman and Phil Knight in Portland, Oregon, in 1964 (initially called Blue Ribbon Sports, the company became Nike in 1978, and later moved to Beaverton, Oregon). Knight was a Stanford graduate with a keen business sense. While at Palo Alto, he penned an essay about the athletic footwear industry; he noted that Japan and other Asian countries were well ahead of the business curve, thanks to their low labor costs. Knight felt that for an American company to compete it would have to do the same—sound capitalist thinking that dominates American business today. However, Knight wrote his essay in 1963, well before the idea of shifting production overseas became as honored as it now is. Little did Knight know that at the time of his essay the Kennedy administration was bombing the piss out of South Vietnam, leading to a decade of imperial violence that would create the labor market of his dreams.

By the late 1970s, Nike had nearly 80 percent of its running shoes made in Asia. The brash young company turned a profit, which led to mainstream approval. C. Ronald Christensen, then dean of the Harvard Business School, hailed

Knight in *The New York Times* as a "corporate pope" who oversaw "lots of apostles and followers." But in this new Vatican sixties guilt lingered. In his book, Jim Naughton wrote that Nike executives were "often children of the Pacific Northwest's counterculture, sensitive to the ethical dilemmas inherent in corporate success." Their devotion to bettering the health of America led to a "strange blindness," according to Naughton. What was it that Nike executives failed to see? That "perhaps 85 percent of their sneakers were not worn in athletic endeavors"; that Nike had become more a fashion symbol and less a part of personal fitness. The company entered the 1980s losing ground, money, and prestige. This, coupled with the rise of Reebok, which catered to women's sports footwear, a market Nike overlooked, led to the company's near destruction.

All fine dramas have a riveting second act, and Nike's was no different. As Reebok grew in strength, matters became grim in Beaverton. Then, in 1985, Nike made the acquaintance of Michael Jordan, a Dean Smith prodigy who was learning the NBA game with the Chicago Bulls. Jordan's agent, David Falk, had already secured for his client deals with Coke and McDonald's; now Falk wanted Jordan to endorse a signature shoe line, something that at the time was not widely done. Several years earlier, Converse had on its payroll Julius Erving, Magic Johnson, and Larry Bird. But these three were proven commodities who helped revive the NBA and made the league a major fan draw. Jordan, though talented, was a kid, and most of the country knew nothing of him nor his on-court potential. But Falk was persuasive;

and the promotion of his star-to-be garnered the interest of Nike, which at that point had very little to lose. Once negotiations ended, Jordan secured a five-year deal worth nearly $2.5 million, royalties included. Toll change today, but then it was the biggest basketball endorsement deal of its kind.

Nike was onboard, yet "they refused to call it the Michael Jordan line," said Falk to Henry Louis Gates, Jr., of *The New Yorker.* "That's when I came up with the idea of calling the shoe Air Jordan, as a compromise between Michael Jordan and Nike." Since Jordan's great years lay ahead, Falk was prescient indeed.* MJ would take to the air again and again, seemingly kicking himself into flight. Only Julius Erving soared from foul line to iron with similiar grace and crowned his descent with a windmill jam or finger-roll layup. But the Doctor was aging; Jordan's younger, sleeker frame allowed for longer hang time, made possible astonishing spins, feints, and shots. Unlike other NBA nicknames—Daryl Dawkins's "Chocolate Thunder," George Gervin's "Iceman," or even Earvin Johnson's "Magic"—there was nothing allegorical about "Air." It literally defined that place where Jordan did the most damage.

Moniker fixed, the time came to lure young consumers. When Jordan joined Nike, the company's national commercial arm was Chiat/Day, one of the "hotter" ad shops of the mid-eighties. The agency made its mark with the *1984*-themed commercial for Apple Computers in which proles

---

*Falk's groundbreaking deals for Jordan made him one of the richest and most celebrated of sports agents. Soon other hot young NBA prospects, from Antoine Walker to Juwan Howard to Allen Iverson to Stephon Marbury, sought his counsel and looked to score even bigger deals than Air.

are freed when a sledgehammer shatters Big Brother's propaganda screen. The spot, aired only once, was hailed as a creative breakthrough, so it seemed fitting that Chiat/Day handle the Air Jordan campaign—"edgy" shop vends emerging brand. The agency linked Jordan directly to his shoe line; no coy, conceptual approach here. To illustrate the Air premise, a playground court became an airport runway. Sound of jet engines. MJ's silhouette glides above a city backdrop, legs apart, ball held in right hand, the arm outstretched. "Who says man was not meant to fly?" asks the Air-borne Bull in voiceover. Certainly not the millions of kids watching at home, glancing at their worn sneakers with disdain.

The desired link was made: Jordan did not merely endorse a shoe, a practice long-polished by other athletes; he and his shoe were one, a union forged in the image of the Jumpman, the name given Jordan's in-flight silhouette. Never before (or really since) did a single frame of an athlete's filmed movement serve as his marketing symbol. Jumpman helped to take Nike out of its sales slump and back to the forefront of athletic footwear promotion and design. And all achieved on the back of a rookie guard for a mediocre team. The execs in Beaverton saw that the future of the company was bound with this self-confident, soft-spoken young Bull, whose potential, both athletic and business, was nowhere near its peak. A variety of new Air models would be sold; new apparel too. This meant that the Air image itself would expand to include other facets of the Jordan experience. Flight alone was not enough.

The second series of Air Jordan spots were conceived by

the ad shop of Wieden & Kennedy. Originally Nike's sole commercial arm, Wieden & Kennedy lost the national account to Chiat/Day in 1983. (Portland-based, W&K maintained its regional duties for Nike.) But Chiat/Day became difficult to deal with. There were creative conflicts, clashes of ego, a lack of trust between partners. Also, sales of Nike shoes failed to rise. So in 1986 Nike got rid of Chiat/Day and Wieden & Kennedy won back its old account. The agency immediately proved its worth by producing the famous Nike spot "Revolution," a black-and-white barrage of physical exertion set to the screams and guitar of John Lennon. The ad was denounced by those who felt it robbed the spirit of sixties music (Bruce Springsteen and John Cougar Mellencamp among them), which it most certainly did; the song's familiar energy drove the images that grabbed consumer eyes. "Revolution" was a brilliant piece of propaganda, equal to Leni Reifensthal's best work—*Olympiad* as scored by the Beatles. It cleared the ground for the next Jordanian wave.

After "Revolution," Wieden & Kennedy added to its arsenal Spike Lee. This too was inspired. Jim Riswold, a W&K creative director, saw Lee's first feature film *She's Gotta Have It*, noticed that Lee's onscreen character Mars Blackmon wore Air Jordans, and visualized a series of spots where Mars and MJ would push the sneakers into the faces of complacent home viewers. This would mark the first real commercial use of blackspeak, not merely as a way to reach an "urban" market but as a fashion statement to excite Caucasian youth. Before Riswold's innovation, black endorsers often followed straight white lines and one could see the strain of, say,

Magic Johnson as he tried "feelin'" 7-Up. The ease with which he ran the Laker fast break vanished on set. But then Magic never ran a commercial break, the reins of which were (and usually are) in smaller, paler hands.

The pale hands guiding the Air Jordan campaign established a different rhythm. Though he wrote what became the "Spike and Mike" spots, Riswold was smart enough to let Lee direct them in the style of *She's Gotta Have It*. This allowed the filmmaker a smooth transition from one form to another and, more importantly, it lent the spots an "authentic" black touch. As Mars, Lee thrust the Air line forward and told you it was the *best* because MJ was the *man*. Pleading and convincing were unnecessary. Mars knew what was down, and in successive commercials he reinforced this claim while Jordan performed his many "patented, vicious" moves. Shot from a variety of angles, crisply edited and frenetic in tone, the "Spike and Mike" ads were a key breakthrough in the promotion of athletic footwear. Riswold and Lee fused the cool and aggressive sides of basketball with humor, energy, and "daring"—the marketing sense of the word, of course. They proved that blackspeak (at least Lee's version of it) was understood, indeed embraced, by white boys; they pushed the ad envelope slightly with indie film techniques; and they helped make Michael Jordan a mass media figure.

Obviously Jordan helped himself on court. The Bulls steadily improved as the eighties progressed and MJ delighted fans with his elegant, high-scoring exhibitions. But Jordan was wise to the necessity of hype, for what is talent if not a means to commercial success? And Jordan, via David Falk, catered shamelessly to those who best turned his skills into gold. McDonald's, Coke, Ball Park Franks, Haynes underwear, Gatorade—all benefited from his image as Great Player/Good Guy. Jordan could be serious, he could be fun, but no matter the mood he seemed like a friendly Negro who was welcome anytime to borrow the lawnmower. Gordon Nye, a vice president at Reebok, said, "The thing about Jordan is that he doesn't alienate anybody." In reference to the Mars Blackmon character in the Nike spots, Jim Riswold added, "The point is here's a guy who is Michael's number-one fan, but he's also a good friend of his. And I think that is the way people feel about Michael."

Mars loved Michael and said so in Brooklyn nigga slang (edited for maximum market punch). But this would never fit Jordan, even though in one ad he assumed Mars's posture and dress, with Fearless Fly glasses and "Do ya know do ya know do ya know?" expression. Clearly a gag, as Jordan was destined for far grander things. "Spike and Mike" did, however, inspire its share of commercial knockoffs, including "Mr. Robinson's Neighborhood" and "Bo Knows," both written by Riswold for Nike. But these, along with the "Grandmama" bits Larry Johnson did for Converse (the former Hornet in spinster drag pounding his way to the glass), remained tongue-in-cheek. Attitude, *black* attitude, a caricature of toughness favored by teens of varied hues, was seen fronting products from Sprite to the Gap. Its minstrel roots made white renditions inevitable, like the through-your-skull spots for PlayStation and Sega. The blackspeak of Mars Blackmon became the chatter of Lil' Penny, the marionette with Chris Rock's mouth who dogged his human namesake on behalf of—who else?—Nike. Make Chris Tucker the voice of a sassy tackling dummy ("Yo punk! Is dat all you *got?!*") and Nike's soul trilogy will be complete.

Despite its attachment to the lighter side of black expression, Nike rattled professional moralists with a stark TV ad in which Charles Barkley claimed, "I am not a role model." A refreshing if calculated admission. One might have thought that such commercial directness would be hailed or at least appreciated. But American celebrities must set good examples; it comes, we are told, with the turf. Once your image goes graven and your bank account swells, it is your duty to "give back" to the kids, to members of your tribe or sect, to all those who cheer you on. Barkley said no; look to parents and teachers for inspiration and guidance. An athlete's job is to play his game to the best of his ability and little else. For this the aging Sun (soon to become a descending Rocket) was slammed by those devoted to mass media uplift. Nike too was critiqued. The concept that someone famous would shirk his "responsibility" did not ease down the moralist gullet. It did, however, give Nike added market "edge" and made Barkley the most notorious Afro-Republican since Clarence Thomas.

As it turned accomplished athletes into clowns and moral relativists, Nike saved its glossiest plans for its valued commodity: Michael Jordan. The early projection of MJ as airline and straight man to Spike Lee gave way in the late eighties to a more nuanced image of strength, grace, and depth. Jordan himself became a stronger all-around player, and his will to win an NBA championship sharpened his competitive streak. This didn't mean that Jordan would now be a humorless hunk: His handlers were too savvy to allow such a thing. But as his legend grew, it was obviously felt that he should look the part of an elite hoops star; that his on-court presence spread into the culture and establish the same firm grip. After the Bulls got past the Pistons and beat Magic's ebbing Lakers squad for their first ring in 1991, the era of God Jordan truly began, his throne the shape of Nike's swoosh.

However, casting Jordan as world deity was too literal an approach, like Gatorade's "If I could be like Mike!" campaign. Here the connection to Jordan was made strictly through a fluid that most people swill when hungover. At best his fans might realize a green-liquid fantasy where with one sip they too would fly above weak switch-offs and abortive double teams . . . but then be slammed to the floor, no foul called. If they really could "be like Mike" the whistle would be blown; but they can't, so they should drink their fucking Gatorade and stay down. Yet this campaign, for all of its flaws, did well and ran for years, while countless Gatorade users stared up from the ground to some dream game in the sky.

Fittingly, it took the lads at Wieden & Kennedy to harness Jordan's power with aikido precision. In "Instant Karma," Jim Riswold's sequel to "Revolution," Jordan appears once with teammate Scottie Pippen and again on his own, and interspersed throughout are flashes of women swimming, an aerobics class, kids doing the double Dutch, soccer players, a guy atop a backboard being pelted with basketballs, a child smiling, a man at a rowing machine, a woman completing her last sit-up. As in "Revolution," the voice heard is John Lennon's; and like the earlier ad, music and images blend most effectively. Every flexed muscle and bead of sweat are boosted by the song's pounding drums and piano. Intermittently placed are title cards with lyric samples like INSTANT and SUPERSTAR. While celeb jocks Michael Johnson and Joannie Benoit also appear, it's obvious who owns the spot though his presence is fleeting. "We all shine on. Like the moon and the stars and the sun," sings Lennon; and the one who shines brightest is the one we barely see.

With "Instant Karma" (directed by David Fincher, who later helmed *Alien*[3] and *Seven*) Nike made its competitors look heavy and slow-witted. Wieden & Kennedy hit an intense creative stride that earned the shop a "sexy" reputation, and their clever use of Jordan in the spot showed their skill in marketing a cultural force. Of course not every Nike ad moved with the finesse of "Karma": "Hare Jordan," in which MJ and Bugs Bunny destroy a team of scrubs, was a frantic attempt to recapture the humor and velocity of classic Warner Bros. cartoons that fell miles from the mark. Jordan was simply not the comic type; but when big money beckons, the idea that the material should fit the talent is snuffed without a second thought. This explains how a painfully unfunny spot like "Hare Jordan" was later expanded for the big screen under the title *Space Jam*. Kids apparently loved watching His Airness tame animated beasts, and the movie's box office receipts and commercial tie-ins proved that Jordan could generate profits while mumbling his way through a Chuck Jones nightmare.

Still, there was a serious Air side, and Wieden & Kennedy fleshed it out in a fine spot where Jordan pondered his almighty status. "What if there were no sports?" he asks, his face a solemn mask. "Where would I be? Who would I be? Would I still be your hero?"* These rhetorical questions were used to encourage those lacking MJ's gifts to help the young get involved with sports—a Nike PSA. Here Jordan seems humble, a lucky guy born into a culture that favors sports stars. Were he born into slavery, he might have been Air Mandingo, forced to fight Ken Norton to amuse James Mason. Were he born into an alternate universe, he might possess one eye, three nostrils, twin mouths, and prune the gelatin shrubs in the cellophane gardens of Orasia. But he was born into this grim world where pro basketball is revered and those who play it best get rich. In the time it takes to pitch diet soda, God Jordan searched his soul and the faith of true believers and found his kingdom intact.

Doubt, reflection, the assessment of different fates are what furrow the brow of this deity. In a later Nike spot, MJ spoke of his difficult climb to the top of the NBA heap. "I've failed over and over again in my life. And that is why I succeed." As he told Henry Louis Gates, Jr., "The idea is to tell young kids, 'Don't be afraid to fail, because a lot of peo-

---

*This "humble" approach was employed by Sprite in a 1999 ad starring Kobe Bryant. Would we mortals drink Sprite, Kobe asks, if he were one of us and washed dishes for a living? Something to ponder when shopping for soda.

ple have to fail to be successful . . .' Let them know that it isn't always good for the people up top. I mean, they have bad things happen to them." But failure for most usually means failure for life, not the minefield one must cross to finally realize success. Coming from Jordan, it sounds almost worth enduring: The shit will taste better washed down with champagne. Yet few really believe they will clink glasses with MJ. His democratic pieties, however sly a ruse, are meaningless. He is beyond conventional reach, fit only for the gaze of admirers. The Air he breathes would suffocate the majority of those lucky enough to inhale it.

In the hypnotic "Frozen Moment," we see Jordan in the proper light: the Godhead who lures mortals into a collective trance. Jordan takes a pass at the top of the key; upon touching the ball, all movement slows to a dreamlike pace. Those watching this "game" on TV slow down as well: health club patrons on treadmills; a man about to shave his lathered face, the sink overflowing with water; a woman and a boy sitting together as a dog shakes water from its coat, unnoticed; a boy staring through a TV store window; another boy viewing a set in his garage as his bike falls onto the driveway. All are mesmerized by Jordan's cut to the basket, spin in the lane, drive for a slam. The intercutting between MJ and the fans is sharp but conforms to the super-slo-mo of the spot, and one wonders how many people watching *this* felt themselves slowing as well.

Jordan's Wieden & Kennedy spots set a standard not only for the industry but for other Nike ads made by the agency. "The ads almost never pitch the product or even mention

Nike's name," boasts the company in its statement, "Main Goals of Nike Marketing." "They create a mood, an attitude, and then associate the product with that mood. It's something called an image transfer." The company then quotes Dan Wieden himself: "We don't set out to make ads. The ultimate goal is to make a connection." How best to do this? One approach was to show the power of television *on* television, as in "Frozen Moment." Also, there's the use of sets as action figures. In "Dueling TVs," one set contains Andre Agassi, the other David Wheaton. Both exchange forehands and backhands so aggressively that their sets fly about a TV repair shop, then collide and shower glass. In a spot for Nike's Air Max, William S. Burroughs, author and firearm artist, appears on another moving TV, reciting stark prose about the future of human expression. In these and similiar ads, the presence of Ernie Kovacs is evident, as is video pioneer Nam June Paik and Timothy Leary's head, its voice heard from behind a freezer door.

When Nike added the San Francisco agency Goodby, Silverstein & Partners to its commercial roster, Wieden's goal of making a connection was richly enhanced. The creators of "Got Milk?" imagined, "What if we treated all athletes the way we treat skateboarders?" Golfers, tennis players, and runners are harassed and kept from course, court, and street by cops who ask, "What do you think you're doing here?" Nike's police state nightmare is not the rounding up of dissidents nor the burning of books, but the criminalization of recreational sports (which would doubtless affect Nike sales). The spots are clever, amusing, and appeal to the casual jock's inner "outlaw"—a toned rogue who plays where he wants as hard as he wants and screw those who don't get it. But Nike got it. The company and its promotional team artfully joined the aggressive and poetic sides of sport. Through its seductive imagery and keen marketing plan, Nike created a mystique that attracted millions devoted to fitness and sweat, as well as youths convinced of their professional destiny.

Nike did more than arouse the swoosh-wearing young: It sponsored basketball camps for high school kids with real hoops potential. But the camps were not an exercise in corporate generosity, a place where the talented few may test one another's skills in a safe, supportive environment. The camps were designed as upscale slave markets, an auction space for America's hardwood plantations. The instincts behind such an idea are hardly new to the sporting world. Young bucks who can leap, shoot, run, and pass are forever needed to replace those who leave the college game and those too old or battered to play in the pros. The meat wheel demands constant tending; and there under Nike's banner are college coaches in search of the firmest, fastest, sleekest chattel the inner cities and rural areas can produce.*

Nike loves to take care of college coaches, and these coaches swear their allegiance in return. Class acts like Duke's Mike Kryzewski, North Carolina's Dean Smith, and

---

*In the brilliant *Hoop Dreams*, we get a peek at one of these camps—white coaches overseeing the young black bodies below them. Most amusing is Spike Lee's cameo where Mr. Knick delivers a Black Power speech to the assembled high school talent. That Lee is a proud Nike flack apparently does not compromise his "militant" stance, but it does provide a few laughs.

Georgetown's John Thompson have all had Nike bucks stuffed in their g-strings, and Thompson's dance was so alluring that the company paid him to be a consultant, placed him on its board of directors, and sold him company stock worth over $2 million. Part of this was public relations: When urban kids began getting shot for their Air Jordans, a respectable black figure had to be bought in order to prove that Nike cared about the safety of its customers. John Thompson filled the bill without shame and happily wore the swoosh to the applause of his coaching peers. Nike's purchase of Thompson helped mute some of the criticism it received on the kids-and-guns front; but there were other, equally deserving coaches and athletic departments in need of lucrative deals.

In the summer of 1997, the University of Kentucky received its share of the pie. The deal was simple: UK was paid to promote Nike. Technically speaking, the agreement was made between the company and the Kentucky Athletic Association, thereby avoiding government involvement, as UK is a state university. But the contract was signed by top university officials who did not need approval from the Board of Trustees, which, given the terms of the agreement, probably would have assented anyway. According to Lowell Reese of the *Kentucky Gazette*, the Nike deal could bring the university "as much as $30 million over the course of the initial five-year contract, which runs from Sept. 1 [1997] through Aug. 31, 2002, with an option to renew." UK would get "$250,000 in cash as an immediate bonus for signing, $6.63 million in cash in five equal annual installments, $3.15 million in free shoes, apparel, and accessories, and up to an estimated $20 million in royalties from the sale of UK merchandise by Nike through its international sports distribution network." Head basketball coach Tubby Smith would receive compensation of around $1 million annually; the football and women's basketball coaches were given deals as well.

What was Nike's taste? As Reese detailed it in his *Gazette* piece, "Nike entered into the deal for two principal reasons: 1) for the national TV and other media coverage that UK basketball receives, and 2) for the accompanying 'prominent brand exposure' Nike will receive by having its logo on UK's uniforms. Every time a Wildcat stands at the foul line to shoot a free throw, it's going to be a potential commercial for Nike." On top of this, the university must "include public address announcements at each home game that will recognize Nike as the exclusive product supplier and sponsor of UK's program." Full-page four-color ads for the company would go into game programs at no charge; the swoosh would be on the seat backs of the home and visitors' benches; and every member of UK's athletic staff, from coaches to varsity players, were to wear Nike shoes, apparel, and accessories—and nothing else. If in the unlikely event a player or coach were to question Nike's business or labor practices, that person would risk his or her job or place on a team. Dissent was not an option.

The NCAA, which placed Kentucky's basketball program on probation in the late 1980s due to recruitment violations, had nothing negative to say about the Nike deal. But then this was a straightforward commercial bribe, perfectly acceptable in a way that sneaky recruiting tactics are not. Besides, similiar deals were struck with other A-list programs across the nation, so who in authority would object? Indeed, the same logic held for the CBS Sports division at the beginning of the 1998 Winter Olympics in Nagano, Japan. To better emphasize Nike's sponsorship of CBS's coverage of the Games, it was decided that network correspondents would wear blue jackets bearing the swoosh. In a parallel universe, on-air personalities like Harry Smith, Mark McEwen, Bill Geist, and Bob Simon would have set fire to the Nike jackets and made public their outrage. But here docility ruled. As the fiftysomething Geist meekly told *The New York Times*, "It was just kind of understood that those were the jackets that we were to wear." Geist said he was bothered by this policy, yet nothing was done until CBS News president Andrew Heyward ordered the jackets removed. Not that Heyward was opposed to Nike sponsoring the Games; he merely seemed embarrassed that CBS staffers were so openly whoring themselves.

Another member of the news division was "dismayed and embarrassed" by the spectacle, but her comments maddened Heyward even more. In October 1996 Roberta Baskin produced a rather damning report on Nike's labor practices in Vietnam for "48 Hours." This naturally galled Nike and slave-labor advocates like *The Wall Street Journal* and the story never reaired. But a year later Baskin discovered a report by Nike's auditors, Ernst & Young, in which the claims made in her "48 Hours" piece regarding the awful working conditions in Vietnam were verified. Based on this corroborating evidence, Baskin wanted to follow up her original Nike exposé but was denied by her bosses. When the swoosh jacket affair occurred in Nagano, Baskin wondered aloud if maybe, just maybe, Nike's sponsorship of the Games had something to do with the deep-sixing of her follow-up report. Heyward erupted: Baskin's charge was "reckless and irresponsible," he said; more importantly, her comments were "potentially injurious to the reputation of CBS News." Guided by the ghosts of Murrow and Severeid, Heyward went on to claim that Baskin's original Nike report was "thin" and was "difficult to bring to air." Yet before the Nagano hubbub, Baskin's piece had been submitted by CBS News for a DuPont Award, a silver baton tossed at eager broadcast journalists each January. But submission is one thing, winning another; and the fact that Baskin did not win the coveted DuPont proved Heyward right. Thicker, easy-to-air stories are better bets.

Heyward's reaction to Baskin was nothing out of the ordinary. In fact, one could travel from CBS News headquarters to the Hawes School in Ridgewood, New Jersey, and find the same values on display. There the students in Maria Sweeney's fourth-grade class had written a play about sweatshops in Asia. The script was critical of Nike, Disney, and McDonald's, and it was hoped that the rest of the student body would be made aware of the conditions in which sneakers, Disneywear, and Happy Meals toys were made. As dress rehearsal neared, the school's principal canceled the play because it was not "age-appropriate." "They were just going around [the school], saying, 'Don't wear these clothes, don't go to Disney,' " said the principal, who was bothered that the script failed to show "all the good things these corporations do." This, plus the criticism Ms. Sweeney's class received from other students confused by the anti-Nike/Disney talk, forced the kids to stage the play in their classroom for their parents. Many of the students were upset, including Han Park, who told a reporter covering the controversy, "It's like I live in a world with no heart"—a lesson that should stick with Han well after his schooldays.

One of the sources used by Ms. Sweeney's class for their play was Roberta Baskin's "48 Hours" report. Had they contacted Andrew Heyward, he probably would have told them to dismiss her ravings, as would have Lee Weinstein, Nike's communications director at the time. "Roberta certainly has a point of view and her bias is well known," he said after she objected to the Nagano stunt. The kids certainly drew on a number of biased sources, including the corporations involved. They also made overtures to Disney honcho Michael Eisner and the Nike Jumpman himself, Michael Jordan. Neither seemed interested in sharing their thoughts on the matter of sweatshops and the extent to which cheap labor has enriched both. For Eisner this made sense; after all, how does Disney's top man tell kids that their WINNIE THE POOH T-shirts are stitched by jailed Chinese dissidents in conditions farm animals would find abusive? Clearly Eisner would be less comfortable dealing with the issue than the fourth graders he might address. But when it comes to pure sweatshop-inspired discomfort, few have wriggled about with the dexterity of His Airness. His best moves to the hole were leaden by comparison.

The entire Michael Jordan/Nike mess has been a mind-blowing display of hypocrisy, cowardice, mendacity, wretchedness, and corruption—in other words, a typical celebrity PR skirmish. It began in 1990 when Jordan was criticized in connection with those kids who were beaten and shot for their Air sneakers. Surely he had something to say about *this*. After all, his name was on the shoes that people were willing to kill for; and his profile was part of the marketing effort that stirred consumerist desire. Did he in any way feel responsible? Well, no, not really. In fact, he was surprised by the commotion. The real problem was that MJ was caught in a promotional web. His image was that of superstar role model, a nice, quiet guy who perfomed miracles on the court and patted kids on the head, all of whom wished to "Be like Mike." After some of them were left shoeless and bleeding in the street, the person they were told to "be like" did little to help them. And while it's true that Jordan wasn't really answerable for these crimes, his image suggested otherwise: That nice guy on TV adored by America's youth now said he had nothing to contribute. At least Charles Barkley made his disclaimer up front.

Jordan's nonresponse to the violence inspired a few critical words from sportswriters, the most aggressive being Phil Mushnick of *The New York Post*. Jesse Jackson piped up as well and called for a consumer boycott of Nike products. Ever obedient to the swoosh, Spike Lee and John Thompson met with one of Jackson's Operation PUSH lieutenants, the

Reverend Tyrone Crider, and attempted to talk him and Jackson out of the boycott. "We both agreed with his cause," said Lee in *Best Seat in the House*; "we thought his tactics were a little heavy-handed. Coach [Thompson] and I told the Reverend Crider what to do, step by step. [Render unto Caesar, brother.] It was Coach, Jordan, and I who had the ear of [Phil] Knight. The Reverend Crider didn't want to hear that noise, and the thing blew up for a while." The boycott went forward but had no effect on Nike's sales. The single problem facing Phil Knight was that of public relations; one of the most powerful voices in black America was denouncing his company, so there was only one thing to do: buy Jesse off. Operation PUSH was given a sizable "donation" from Nike, after which the good Reverend became more "constructive" in his remarks about the company and its prime symbol, Michael Jordan.

Throughout this minor intrigue, Jordan hid from view. His agent David Falk said that MJ didn't want to become "a pawn" of those with political grievances and was not in support of the boycott. Spike Lee stepped forward to defend his famous buddy and himself. "The Nike commercials that Michael Jordan and I do have never gotten anyone killed," he stated in a letter to *The National,* a former sports daily. Later, in his book, Lee took a few moments to reflect on the issue. "You can't brush that kind of stuff off, like some lint from your shoulder," he said of the reported violence. "Those charges and the realities of day-to-day living make you pause and think." At least until Nike wants the controversy defused and expects you to help do just that. Lee paid lip service to the topic while remaining loyal to his brand and those who disapproved were—what else?—night riders setting aflame his humble shack. Lee's behavior during this time was amusing and instructive. His desire to keep big Nike bucks in his bank account overrode his "concern" that the Man cared nothing for the lives of black youth. Instead, it was Nike's *critics* who were the racists, not Martin Luther Knight engaged in his sneaker crusade.

Nike and Jordan apologists insisted that the Air campaign was aimed at a larger demographic than the "urban" one, namely white kids drawn to phat beats and myriad Afro-delights. You didn't see Cameron shoot Tyler for *his* sneakers, unlike the various Maliks and Snoops bustin' caps in da 'hood. What's a shoe company to do? Jordan's biographer, Jim Naughton, pushed this point even further in his book. Like the "Spike and Mike" spots, Jim Riswold's "Mr. Robinson's Neighborhood," which starred Spurs center David Robinson, had an inner-city appeal. After all, both campaigns featured black men who played basketball and wore Nikes, a winning mix. Yet "Mr. Robinson" spoke primarily to whites because it was based on the PBS children's show, which, as Naughton reminded us, is not a "major force in the ghetto." (Actually, the premise was lifted from Eddie Murphy's parody of "Mister Rogers' Neighborhood" on "Saturday Night Live.") So if Nike wasn't pitching Robinson's shoe to a demographic where poverty, unemployment, and crime rates are high, why would it bother to do so with the more popular (and more expensive) Air Jordans? Despite the white references in its commercials, Nike, as do most companies, looks to sell its merchandise to *anyone* who can cough up the dough. Besides, the idea that those "in the ghetto" do not watch or understand shows like "Mister Rogers' Neighborhood" is ridiculous, given the reach of mass media and the cultural hybrids that emerge from the din.

The combination of hush money, denial, and media diversion worked to Nike's advantage; the controversy faded from view, and the question of whether or not there was a link between the creation of desire and the violent means to satisfy said desire was altogether dropped. Although Nike spun brilliantly on its own behalf, the fact was that the majority of the press and other media cared little for the issue. Black kids killing each other? So what's new? Nike was a class act, employed the best in advertising and public relations, promoted the country's top athletes with style and imagination. Not many journalists or commentators will rip apart this scenario, especially since they inhabit the same media space where Nike does business.

Given this leeway, the Nike gang grew arrogant and assumed (somewhat correctly) that everyone in the media shared their values, thus their bid to outfit CBS correspondents in swoosh couture. The gang also grew intolerant of any fun made at their expense. Nike lawyers demanded that Candie's Inc. stop using the line "Just Screw It" in its ads that featured the blonde satirist Jenny McCarthy wearing its low-priced sneakers. This, Nike felt, was too close to Dan

Wieden's sacred and immensely popular "Just Do It," and was therefore off-limits, even in jest.* Candie's resisted and the issue was left to the lawyers. Nike then went after NBC for its parody of the company's less-successful "I can" campaign. To promote yet another sitcom, this one called "Working," NBC changed the Nike image of sweat and achievement to one of foolishness and sloth. "I can photocopy my face," said the show's main character. "I can sleep with my eyes open." Here Nike met with no resistance. Its executives told NBC that "I Can" was a new campaign and asked if, as a professional courtesy, the network would stop making jokes. NBC did. But instead of letting the matter drop there, Nike piously claimed that its "I Can" spots conveyed optimism and made life a bit nicer for all. NBC's parody was "cynical," said Nike spokeswoman Kathryn Reith, who added, presumably straight-faced, "We think there is plenty of cynicism in the world."

Nike was in a position to know. In the midst of its many PR efforts, the company received criticism for the conditions in which its shoes were made overseas. The initial complaints, however, came not from the press but from labor, student, and human rights groups. As far as most of the media were concerned, Nike made great shoes and cool commercials. But for those who saw firsthand the misery of women—and sometimes children—forced to work sixteen to twenty hours a day for next to nothing, the image of Nike

---

*Some believe that Wieden, ad genuis though he is, appropriated this classic line from the choreographer George Ballanchine, who told generations of his dancers, "Don't think about it. *Just do it.*"

was tarnished. The trick was to get media outlets to amplify this image for a national audience.

Predictably, it took a celebrity scandal to bring American press attention to the problem. When it was revealed that Kathie Lee Gifford's clothing line for Wal-Mart was made in Honduran sweatshops where all manner of abuse was commonplace, Kathie Lee denied any wrongdoing and threatened to sue those who raised the issue. Friends like the composer John Tesh publicly sided with her and the story became tabloid fodder. But once the facts rolled in, Kathie Lee teared up, apologized for being misled, and said she'd rectify the mistake. She sent husband Frank to distribute $9,000 in cash to garment workers in Manhattan who also toiled on her behalf. She met with Labor Secretary Robert Reich and later testified before a congressional panel, where she spoke of her humanity and sensitivity to pain and injustice. She called for better working conditions for those who stitched her clothing line; and if necessary, the jobs would go to another country where rights were respected and pay was decent.

The spotlight on Kathie Lee quickly spread to Michael Jordan and Nike, and here the show got ugly. For one thing, Jordan lacked Kathie Lee's instinct for survival. Were she on the dock at Nuremberg, Kathie Lee would escape the noose by painting herself as a Dauchau waif, misguided and lost in her own good intentions. Few can mesh anguish, outrage, and self-pity as skillfully as Kathie Lee, then put it to commercial use. She understands better than most the shifting winds of celebrity and adapts accordingly. Jordan, on the other hand, is dazed whenever his celebrity is questioned.

His usual malapropisms, which were in full flower during postgame interviews, ebb as his face registers confusion and anger. He never quite says, "Do you know who I *am*?" but then he doesn't have to. The glare he gave refs who dared called him for a foul said that and more.

The reason for these rare but cutting looks stems from the fact that Jordan endures almost no real press scrutiny.* Since ascending to his throne, MJ has grown accustomed to journalists kissing his feet (his ass was reserved for his teammates); so when the sweatshop furor erupted, he was of course stunned that his name was brought up. He uttered a few lame denials—"I think that's Nike's responsibility . . . I don't know the complete situation. Why should I? I'm trying to do my job"—but unlike Kathie Lee, who defends her honor with a badger's intensity, Jordan usually skips direct confrontation and relies on his cronies to settle matters. In the case of Nike's sweatshops, however, matters were not so easily settled—or dismissed.

David Stern gave it a shot. The NBA commissioner scolded those who expected Jordan to respond to the charges in some meaningful way. To hold His Airness responsible for Third World labor abuses was in Stern's estimation unfair. Stern's defense of the league's top draw was purest dam-

---

*The single instance when Jordan was scrutinized off-court was for his gambling, a habit that crippled the careers and reputations of other star athletes like Denny McLain and Pete Rose. But Jordan, taking bets on private links, escaped serious damage. There are some conspiracy buffs who believe that MJ's first "retirement" was arranged with David Stern to lessen the heat of this scrutiny; that there was no doubt that Jordan would return to the Bulls, making himself and the NBA even more lucrative. If true, this was a masterstroke of marketing genius that would cause monkeys to thrust themselves blind.

age control. The NBA could not have as its ambassador a man who knowingly made $20 million off the misery of the powerless, so the best tactic was to plead ignorance on his behalf and repeat his claim that he was a simple ballplayer doing his job. Stern himself held two jobs: 1) NBA chieftain; and 2) advance man for the Michael cult. It was in this latter capacity that Stern attempted to deny that someone as good and pure as Jordan would be connected to something so *wrong*. The guy loves kids, for God's sake! Though seemingly calm as he flacked away, Stern must have experienced a wicked adrenaline surge as images of a slave master Michael reeled through his brain: the future Hall of Famer riding the backs of Asian teens, pearly whites sunk into long, yellow necks . . . Who knows? Maybe that's how Air spent his vacations. But Stern lived up to his surname and deflected attention elsewhere. When attention fell on Nike, the company was prepared. Or so it was assumed.

At this point, Nike got away with so much that its executives saw the sweatshop problem as a mere PR speedbump. This thinking was reflected in their public statements. First of all, the sweatshops were not owned by Nike but were "subcontracted" to Korean and Taiwanese nationals who "managed" the Indonesian and Vietnamese girls stitching the shoes. "There's some things we can control and some things we can't control," said Phil Knight, regarding his Asian partners in crime. If the girls are beaten, humiliated, forbidden to go to the bathroom or to speak, given two cups of water per shift, and forced to work overtime for a half cup of rice, then hey! Can't blame us! Not our factory! It was a spirited defense effort. Knight and his crew maintained that since Nike wasn't *directly* involved with these foreign operations, they were absolved of any human rights violations. That the company would later market the shoes and collect the profits was not viewed by Knight as a contradiction of his claims, nor as hypocrisy. Moreover, he expected the media to buy this line of thought; and while Knight was respectfully quoted (especially in the business press), not even the most dedicated NAFTA hack could ignore the eyewitness testimony emanating from Southeast Asia. Thus Knight's evasions were often placed next to the pleas of Nike critics, one of whom said to *Business Week* in July 1996, "for workers on the inside, it's hell."

Once Knight's initial rationale bit the dust, he shifted to an earlier, effective tactic: paying a recognized "moral" figure to hand Nike a clean bill of health. And who better to deem the shoe company a leader in civil rights than a veteran of that very struggle, the spotless Andrew Young. Here was a guy, a man of *God*, who taught young activists the means to register black voters in the South; who was one of Martin Luther King, Jr.'s trusted associates; who, as Jimmy Carter's ambassador to the United Nations, was one of the first high American officials to recognize Palestinians as humans (for which the *schwartze* was canned). "Why, who could possibly question Andrew Young's integrity?" asked a Nike publicity manager of Nat Hentoff, a *Village Voice* columnist. Hentoff could and did, as did many human rights groups. To what did they all object? After Young toured twelve of Nike's "contracted" factories in Vietnam, China, and Indonesia in March and April 1997, he released a report that exonerated the company of "widespread systemic abuse or mistreatment of workers." The factories were "clean, organized, adequately ventilated, and well lit." Shortcomings existed; nothing is perfect. But overall, Phil Knight had no reason to lose sleep, assuming he lost any to begin with.

Nike's critics were not appeased. "We were hoping that Andrew Young would come out with something significant. But this report is meaningless," said Medea Benjamin of Global Exchange, a human rights group in San Francisco. A few of Young's former colleagues in the civil rights movement, now members of the Campaign for Labor Rights, sent a letter to Nike's newest apologist, written, as they put it, "in sadness" more than anger. "Your report is a betrayal of the principles for which Dr. King gave his life in Memphis where he made his last public appearance in support of a sanitation workers' strike—the right of workers to organize free trade unions, to be recognized and to gain dignity in the workplace." They mocked Young's contention that Nike wasn't responsible for the abuses because of its "subcontracting" arrangement with Asian factories. "Doesn't that sound something like the sharecropping system?" asked his onetime associates. Young never answered. But Nike's vice president of law and corporate affairs, Lindsay D. Stewart, did: "There's no way any report would convince the human rights groups, who are saying Andrew Young has been bought, of something other than their biased beliefs." Had Young delivered a blistering attack on all that Nike believed

true—on its dime, no less—the unbiased company would certainly have publicized and defended it with similar gusto.

Among the items glossed over by Young were, of course,
the low wages paid for spine-bending labor (no lower than
what other American companies pay in the region, said
Nike); the illegality of workers to form unions and engage in
collective bargaining (what? and force corporations to find even
cheaper labor in more desperate countries?); and the environ-
mental hazards faced by workers unable to adequately protect
themselves. This was most evident in some of Nike's Vietnam
factories where shoes were assembled with the chemicals ace-
tone and toluene, the latter of which ravages the central nervous system and causes birth defects—just like the good old
days when American chemical know-how killed and de-
formed zipperheads by the bushel. According to *The New
York Times,* Nike kept this tradition alive by allowing carcin-
ogen levels to reach 177 times the legal limit in Vietnam, a
"limit" etched in dust and kicked up by corporations fleeing
communist EPA laws in the United States. To Phil Knight's
and Andrew Young's probable relief, the majority of the mass
media did not follow up the *Times* piece, although ESPN aired
a moderately critical report twice in April 1998. The all-sports
network hit both Nike and Reebok on the issues of abuse and
toxins in the workplace, while Adidas sensibly refused to coop-
erate. Never let them see your sweatshop, the PR boys advise.*

---

*A few months later, Adidas was accused of using Chinese political prison-
ers in Shanghai to make its World Cup '98 soccer balls. In a $1.2 billion
lawsuit filed by Chinese dissidents, the prisoners were "coerced" into making the balls "under inhumane conditions," including being beaten with
belts and other "tortures of various horrifying kinds." Faced with increas-
ing pressure, Adidas announced that it would cease using prisoner labor.

Amid these and other semipublic controversies, Michael Jordan cashed his Nike checks in silence as his lackeys kept a noble front. Fans were told of Jordan's many charities and personal causes like battling cancer in children and, with wife Juanita, establishing the M&J Endowment Fund to support community outreach, including shelters for battered women. Naturally these efforts were reserved for American victims of disease and domestic violence; that Jordan quietly profited from the work of foreign women exposed to cancer-causing agents and violent foremen meant relatively nothing to those marveling at his humanity. In fairness, one must note that in 1995 Jordan *did* fight for better and more lucrative working conditions for that abused underclass of workers, NBA players. The owners demanded a salary cap; Jordan and his comrades resisted. Here MJ was "a working-class hero," as Larry Platt of *Details* put it, and the players staved off the owners' thuggish demands until the more serious confrontation in 1998 that led to a lockout and a minor reprisal of Jordan's labor activism.* In the meantime, Jordan sold more Nike sneakers and Gatorade and told kids to avoid drugs and to stay in school.

Despite all this, Jordan's critics continued their sniping: When would he speak out about Nike? Enter Jesse Jackson, again. The Rev, who years earlier urged Jordan to address the effects Nike's ads had on the poor, now said that athletes, especially superstars, were unfit to talk politics or policy. "That is not what they are really qualified to do," he intoned.

---

*Performed grudgingly. Jordan knew by this time that he was not returning to the Bulls and so remained clear of confrontation. After all, what would *he* get out of it?

"[T]he issue of trading with Indonesia with regard to human rights or child labor is fundamentally a matter that United States trade policy must address. It isn't right to shift the burden to [Jordan] because he's a high-profile spokesman." One can see Jackson making a similar point to Jesse Owens before the 1936 Berlin Olympics; or to John Carlos and Tommie Smith before they raised their gloved fists in Mexico City; or to Muhammad Ali as he defied the draft board that wished to send him to Vietnam. Of course, Nike money had nothing to do with Jesse's one-eighty. The spirit that led him to pray with and defend Bill Clinton during the President's impeachment was the one he used to shield Jordan from further reproach.

In a 1998 *New Yorker* profile of His Airness, Henry Louis Gates, Jr., lifted a modest shield as well. When discussing how "discomfitting" the Nike controversies were for Jordan, Gates was awed by how he "handled the situations with considerable skill, chastising neither the company nor its critics" and gave him points for nimbly "sidestepping political controversy." Of course, there were those, like NFL legend Jim Brown, who found Jordan lacking social awareness. But then, MJ "has never sacrificed himself to a political cause in the way Muhammad Ali did . . ." (Of course not. Can anyone imagine Jordan taking the ethical stand that Ali took in resisting a criminal war, especially if that stance derailed his career?) Still, Jordan had a few political bones in his body. He told Gates that he would support a Colin Powell presidential run (an interesting link, given the old soldier's involvement in Vietnam), and that he was distressed by the low number of blacks in professions like medicine and law. But no matter his concerns, Jordan remained above it all in "the crow's nest of popular culture," as Gates put it, to reflect on his power and the uncertainty therein.

A number of Jordan's reflections were captured in an illuminating and self-serving piece for *ESPN Magazine* that same year. Here Jordan answered his critics (to Jesse's consternation?) and made public his musings on celebrity, sport, and the stress and importance of being Michael. Regarding Nike, Jordan said that his silence was personal; the company never put him up to it. As for the people who assembled his shoes, Jordan announced, "I want to go to Southeast Asia to see the Nike plants for myself. I really do. I plan on doing it. Should I have done it earlier? No, because I wasn't at the stage of my career where I could make decisions like that away from the game." Certainly Nike would be thrilled to have its top moneymaker tour its Asian sites: The commercial tie-ins alone would justify the trip, complete with film of MJ smiling and nodding down to Nike's Vietnamese translators ("She says, 'I love Nike more than food!' "), signing autographs and helping to dispose of faulty sneakers by jump shooting them into trash bins.

Jordan promised that once he retired he would take a "bigger stand in social and political things. I look at someone like Jackie Robinson, and I see that he became a lot more outspoken after he left the game." Air's use of Robinson as a retired role model is telling. After all, it was Robinson who criticized blacks protesting the Vietnam War, primarily Muhammad Ali, whose refusal to join the gook fry overseas galled the former Dodger. A veteran of World War II whose son served and was wounded in 'Nam, Robinson was of the generation that saw every American fight as one for freedom. But he was also beholden to the dominant white culture that plucked him from the Negro League and made possible his pioneer—and star—status. One should recall his reluctance to denounce Paul Robeson, who said that American blacks had no call ever to fight the Soviet Union. Robinson was pressured to counter this with the claim that most Negroes were law-abiding and patriotic, so Robeson didn't know what he was talking about. (Robeson, however, *did* know the score and never held a grudge against Robinson.) It's been said that Robinson's opinions were not only rooted in the need to please the powerful, but stemmed from a rage he suppressed in his first season with the Dodgers when he shook off death threats, cheap shots and racial slurs with a businesslike demeanor.

It's unlikely that Jordan will ever publicly trash another athlete who bucks the status quo. He's far too careful and self-centered to do such a thing. Yet for Jordan to say he's inspired by Robinson suggests that he sits on some rage of his own, a shred of it directed at those in the press who have failed to give the Bull God their complete and abject devotion. Granted, the number of nonbelievers is small, but a few have dared question MJ's divinity. When Jordan first quit basketball in 1993 to pursue his baseball fantasy, *Sports Illustrated* advised in a headline: BAG IT, MICHAEL! JORDAN AND THE WHITE SOX ARE EMBARRASSING BASEBALL.

This rather simple and accurate observation was seen by

Jordan as disrespect of the lowest order. "I haven't talked to them since they had that cover," he declared in his rambling *ESPN* piece, "and I'm going to hold to it. What they said was totally wrong. Totally wrong. They didn't even have an understanding of the situation. I mean, if they would have at least investigated things, they would have known what I was doing. But they made their own assumption. I mean, isn't America all about trying? The other day I saw Garth Brooks trying to play baseball. And he's older than me, isn't he?"

Apart from the Garth Brooks non sequitur (did he quit country music to play pro ball?), Jordan's rant was fueled by nothing more than hurt pride and the reality of a fantasy ended. Investigate things? Jordan played thirteen exhibition games with the Chicago White Sox and hit a pitiful .150 in twenty appearances at the plate (three singles, no RBIs). Any other prospect would be flushed; but this was His Airness, so off to Double A he went. In a full season for the Birmingham Barons, he hit .202, the lowest batting average that year in the Southern League. Indeed, his strikeout average was eighty-two points higher than his batting average. His speed allowed him to steal thirty bases, but he was thrown out eighteen times. At bottom, Jordan could not play professional baseball.* *Sports Illustrated* was on target and so for-

---

*In his book *Why Michael Couldn't Hit,* Dr. Harold L. Klawans contends that Jordan was past the "critical period" for his nonverbal motor skills to develop and flourish; i.e., he was too old to suddenly hit major or minor league pitching with any consistency. Jordan himself said, "I think I would have been a major league player if I'd played baseball all along." Given his physical skills and determination, probably; but could he then switch to NBA ball in his early thirties having not played the game in nearly twenty years?

bidden from approaching the throne. No matter; there were plenty of followers lounging at His feet, including Larry Platt of *Details,* who trumpeted Jordan's achievements on the diamond. MJ hit "a respectable .260 over the last month of his season," wrote Platt in a nice bit of revisionism, "and was fifth in the Southern League in stolen bases."* Respectable numbers for Chico Escuela, perhaps, but not for one looking to match the twin sports feats of Bo Jackson and Dieon Sanders.

As bad as *Sports Illustrated* made him feel, Jordan's true rage was reserved for the two-headed monster called The Jerrys. GM Krause and owner Reinsdorf did their utmost to piss off their franchise player, either through low pay or what Jordan considered bad management. Yet he remained, partly out of loyalty to Phil Jackson and a love for the city of Chicago, but also because he knew that the Bulls had the chemistry best suited for his talents. After he helped to deliver five NBA championships in seven years, Jordan was finally paid a salary equal to his market worth: some $34 million for the 1997–98 season. But this was not enough. MJ also wanted Reinsdorf's gratitude or a related sign that the Bulls' owner venerated #23. Nothing came. In fact, once the deal was closed, Reinsdorf, according to Jordan, shook his hand and said, "At some point in time, I know I'm going to regret what we just did." Jordan was stunned. Regret? For what? It was *he* who made money for Reinsdorf, who over time raised the

---

*Platt is one of the more creative Jordan apologists in the media. In a September 14, 1999 *Salon* piece, he argued that Jordan's accumulation of wealth was in fact a new form of civil rights activism—despite it coming at the expense of Third World workers.

team's worth from $9.2 million to well over $200 million. *Regret!* "That hit me so deep inside," confessed Jordan, "that sense of greed, of disrespect for me."

Disrespect from a mere real estate mogul is one thing; but it is somewhat ironic that Jordan, of all people, would look down on greed. No American sports figure better understands the power of the dollar than he, and few have hustled the American consumer with greater energy. Reinsdorf may be cheap and enjoy aggravating the help, but the masters of capital appreciate Jordan. His face made the cover of *Fortune* (fuck you, *SI*), and within its pages we learned that over his career MJ has generated $10 billion in revenues. The big chunks were earned for Nike ($2.6 billion in product sales, though analysts place his total effect on the company at $5.2 billion) and the NBA itself ($366 million in television revenues, $3.1 billion in licensing fees). The rest of the ledger is made up of endorsement deals, books, *Space Jam* ($230 million box office, $209 million video), and Michael Jordan Cologne, which raked in $155 million. Apparently, a fair number of men start their day with the scent that drove opposing players crazy. As for the Scent Master himself, he is a modest profit machine, the product of "an old-school upbringing with an emphasis on respect, humility, and a strong work ethic," according to *Fortune*. He is "Everyman," "Superman," the "$10 billion man" who "is not greedy, just fiercely competitive—in any arena."

Generate big money and sainthood is yours, at least until the first profitless quarter. Yet it seems the golden halo will remain with Jordan for some time. His endorsement deal with Nike, which gave the Jumpman his own division, runs through 2025—assuming, of course, that Nike survives until then. The fluctuations of Asian markets and the fashion tastes of American teens wreaked minor havoc on the company in fiscal 1998, when Nike shares fell 20 percent. Phil Knight was thus forced to cut his salary to $1.68 million, the CEO version of a slave wage. This perhaps sensitized him to the plight of sweatshop workers, and in May of that year he declared that Nike would lessen their load. "The Nike product has become synonymous with slave wages, forced overtime, and arbitrary abuse," he said, beard moist with tears. The swoosh would ban child labor, clean the toxic factories air, switch from cancer-causing toluene to water-based solvents to bond the shoes, guard against physical punishment, but would not give the workers a living wage. (Knight wouldn't endure that large a pay cut.) The new standards were announced to great fanfare—and skepticism. Not every Nike critic was convinced of Knight's sincerity. After all, when Knight announced these changes, he maintained that no real abuse ever occurred. His PR flacks later did the same. The effect was comical but in the long run inspired: If Nike truly does clean up its overseas act and insists nothing was ever wrong to begin with, perhaps future consumers will be spared the shameful history.*

---

*However, Nike did all it could to undermine human rights efforts in Vietnam while it publicly and quite shamelessly claimed to support them. On January 11, 1999, a company vice president Joseph Ha sent a private message to a high-ranking Vietnamese labor official that read, in part, "A few U.S. human rights groups, as well as a Vietnamese refugee who is engaged in human rights activities [Thuyen Nguyen of Vietnam Labor Watch], are not friends of Vietnam." Nike, Ha asserted, was, and backed the Vietnamese regime's battle against "subversion." When the message was published in a state-run paper then leaked to the BBC and the *Financial Times,* Nike of course disowned Ha's views and congratulated itself on its devotion to decency and fairness in the workplace.

Regardless of Nike's fortunes, Jordan should remain unaffected. In August 1998, his handlers told potential suitors that Air would promote their products for no less than $2 million per year for ten years. "I am always looking for new endorsement opportunities for Michael," said David Falk, "although in the past five to seven years we have become increasingly selective in the types of deals and relationships we think are appropriate for him." As his numbers have shown, whatever Jordan pitches consumers dutifully buy: Hanes underwear, Sara Lee cakes, and Ball Park franks reached the top spot in their respective markets, thanks to the presence of MJ. Commercial giant that he is, Jordan's greatest success remains his reshaping of the NBA. Falk again: "In tennis or golf or boxing, the mystique is the individual, whereas, no matter how great Bill Russell or Bob Cousy was, it was the Celtic dynasty—it was always institutional. Michael changed all that. Single-handed. Today, when the NBA markets the teams, it says, 'Come watch Penny Hardaway and the Orlando Magic [now, the Phoenix Suns]; come watch Grant Hill and the Detroit Pistons.' Ten years ago, the NBA resisted doing that. It was just that Michael's force was so overwhelming."

So much so that as the 1997–98 season closed with another Bulls championship, onlookers steeled themselves for Jordan's final exit. His Airness toyed with his subjects, hinted at staying on, though it was certain he would leave . . . This year? Next year? Who really knew? He stated firmly he would play only for Phil Jackson, who promptly blew town once the sixth title was secured. Then the lockout, then the wait.

But before the league came to a halt, much noise was made on the subject of Jordan's retirement. To the uninitiated, it must have resembled a religious freakout of sorts—the followers babbling as their Messiah prepared to ascend to his kingdom—and at times this seemed literally the case. Toward the end of the '98 Finals, CNN-SI ran a photo montage of MJ triumphant to the strains of the "Hallelujah Chorus." One may have been tempted to view this as a satirical send-off; but given the cultish nature of the domestic farewells to Jordan, one knew it was an earnest expression of "Thanks for the memories . . ." When it comes to cherished symbols, many Americans have little patience for wisecracks, or worse, sanity.

After the '98 Finals, *Time* asked the question on every sports fan's lips: Was Jordan finally through? The glossy rag couldn't provide the answer—who then could?—but its reporter Joel Stein did his best to keep the Jordan faithful happy with a profile that was, in the glorification of its subject, equal to some of the livelier Kim Il Sung tributes found in the North Korean press. Why do we love MJ? Said Stein, "His will to power is what has kept us on his side after all these years . . . Other than winning with supreme self-assuredness, Jordan is loved because his image is, above all else, personality-less." A clumsy if sincere observation. And just what *is* a "personality-less" person? A "vessel into which America can pour anything it wants." We want Jordan to be "noble, charming, righteous and kind," therefore, he is. According to Stein, Jordan is slicker than Ronald Reagan at his peak, more naturally heroic than John Wayne, and a near-mythological figure on the level of Ulysses. On top of all this, the man at thirty-five could still beat the majority of NBA guards off the dribble and sink shot after picturesque shot. "And he's so cute," added teammate Bill Wennington, an appraisal seconded by Stein.

As if this wasn't enough, the same issue of *Time* included a piece by David Halberstam, who was then completing his book *Michael Jordan: The Making of a Legend,* in which the author known for his studies of the civil rights movement (the most recent being *The Children*) was to establish Jordan's place in American history. While not as smitten as Stein, Halberstam applauded Jordan's greatness—the price of admission when dealing with the man—then illustrated his tireless work ethic, his on-court determination, and the adjustments he made to his game as he aged. Halberstam closed with the commonly held opinion that we may not see anyone like Jordan again, "anyone with that great and complete game." Unlike the endless hosannas found in *Time* and elsewhere, Halberstam's tone suggested he had a fuller understanding of Jordan's rise to Air status. When his book was excerpted months later in *Vanity Fair,* readers were finally given a glimpse of that deeper view.

Although quite favorable to his subject (would MJ tolerate anything less?), Halberstam nevertheless exposes Jordan's mad desire to win at anything, whether it was pool, golf, or even Monopoly. Losing angered him (he was known to upset the Monopoly board when behind, sending the pieces flying) and drove him to improve his game. Halberstam cites sibling rivalry as the root cause of Jordan's mania. For years he was

dominated by his brother Larry, their backyard games of one-
on-one "nothing less than fierce athletic combat." When Michael finally grew taller and became stronger than Larry, the
payback began and, apparently, nourishes his competitive
streak to this day. There was nothing stoic about the way
Jordan chose to improve himself. His was the drive born of
envy and excessive pride, characteristics that many Americans find appealing, and in certain cases, like Jordan's, admi-
rable. There is no honor in second place; so whatever it takes
to come out on top is acceptable. In America, the ends almost
always justify the means, piety notwithstanding. That Jordan
so artfully personifies this belief makes it—and him—all the
more attractive.

Again, Halberstam did not mean to be critical of Jordan.
He showed us the rough side of the legend so that we could
see how MJ was shaped by his mentors—most significantly,
Dean Smith. It was in Chapel Hill where Jordan not only
learned to play the tenacious defense that rounded out his
brilliant offensive skills (and would later make him one of
the top defenders in the NBA), but also where he first ad-
justed his moral compass. Under the guidance of Coach
Smith, whose reputation as a decent guy has never been
questioned, Jordan was instilled with, in Halberstam's words,
"a sense of right and wrong and of how you were supposed
to behave in life." To illustrate this sense of rightness, Halberstam told of a time when Jordan and a friend drove to
Chapel Hill to see a preseason Tar Heels game. Since the
stadium lot was full, Jordan's friend suggested he park his
car in a handicapped space. Jordan refused. "If Coach Smith

ever knew I had parked in a handicapped zone," he said, "he'd make me feel terrible—I wouldn't be able to face him." No doubt Jordan's dread of offending Smith was genuine, and it was nice that a professional basketball star chose not to steal from his physical lessers. But even in this warm anecdote we see the part of Jordan that allows him to profit from misery. He doesn't refuse the handicapped space because it would simply be *wrong* to do so: He fears retribution from an authority figure. Without the mental image of Dean Smith lecturing him on his trangression, Jordan might very well have taken that parking space. Lord knows, he's taken from people worse off than handicapped drivers.

Halberstam's weight as an American chronicler adds to Jordan's status as cultural icon. But the ultimate tribute to Jordan came, fittingly, from Jordan himself. In the fall of 1998, just in time for Christmas (and as a balm for those Bulls fans affected by the lockout), *For the Love of the Game: My Story* appeared in bookstores. As a monument to self-love, *My Story* shines. Could it have been otherwise? When one has been told how great one is year in, year out, one's ego is bound to be affected. That Jordan's greatness lies primarily in his athletic gifts is apparently not enough; he must also be a great person, and this he believes, or wants his audience to believe. Jordan speaks of his life and career as though every detail holds dramatic tension for the reader. From his brushes with death as a boy to his attempts to fit in as an NBA rookie to his relationship with Phil Jackson, MJ brings us in on the deal. Had he wanted to go the full nine, he would have set down his experiences in the third person: "Michael's life was changing and the way Michael was perceived was changing, too. Michael was a father and a husband at home, but everywhere else Michael was MICHAEL JORDAN . . ." First-person singular is far too modest a device for someone as Important as Jordan. Where was David Falk in the editing process?

Lest anyone fret, Jordan tells us that retirement will agree with him. He'll be ever busy, whether designing Nike footwear or skiing some private slope; and if, after all this, he decides to sleep in, that's good too. "As long as I live in the moment, I don't believe I will ever get bored," he says. "I am not going to mind being out of the spotlight." The question here is: Will consumers and fans mind him being out of the spotlight? And how will this affect sales for those companies who employ Jordan as spokesman? For students of marketing and celebrity, the years immediately ahead should be instructive. The force a personality has once he abandons that which defined him has never truly been measured—at least by multimedia standards. Since Jordan has finally retired, his may be the first test case.

The lockout offered a glimpse of him hawking goods as a civilian, and judging by the ads for MCI Long Distance, he was definitely off to a rough start. Surrounded by Warner Bros. cartoon characters in yet another cross-promotion for *Space Jam* ("Own it today!"), His Airness seemed dazed. Playing straight man to Taz and Tweety Bird is not his strong suit, and one trusts that Jordan will again star in something comparable to "Revolution" or perhaps "Frozen Moment," for it is there, in the moment, where he is most comfortable

and effective. Although lacking the punch of those two classic spots, Jordan's appearance in Gatorade's "Is *It* In You?"
ad, where he competes with U.S. soccer star Mia Hamm to
the strains of "Anything You Can Do, I Can Do Better," was
reminiscent of his early Wieden & Kennedy work. Or maybe
he'll assume Cosby's role as Friendly Black Endorser to white
America. Beyond that, what? A sitcom? More movies? NBA
commissioner? Anything goes so long as he, and we, avoids
boredom. And that's all any decent American fan can ask.

Post Game

In the film *Buffalo '66,* Vincent Gallo stages a murder-suicide. His character, Billy, wants to kill a former Bills placekicker (based on Scott Norwood) who missed the winning field goal in a Super Bowl that Billy bet ten grand on. Since he has no money to pay the gangster who took his bet, Billy must take the fall for one of the gangster's cronies or face dire consequences. He is imprisoned for five years. Upon release, he seeks revenge. He finds the Norwood character, whom he blames for his torment, in a strip club. He stands before the guy, fondles his handgun, prepares for the plunge.

Billy imagines what will happen. After he shoots the placekicker and himself, he is buried in some nondescript plot. His parents visit his gravesite, yet his mother (Angelica Huston) is consumed not with grief but with anxiety as she listens to a Bills game on a radio. The game is closer than she would like. A nail-biter. To her, a Bills loss is worse than the loss of her son. Seeing this, Billy abandons his plan. He returns to his cheap hotel room without shooting the Norwood character and nuzzles Christina Ricci.

Gambling, murderous thoughts, fanaticism. Here in a small indie feature do three strands of the contemporary fan experience mesh, scored by the music of Yes. Yet apart from the madness displayed by Houston's character (her home is a mausoleum devoted to the glory of the Bills), *Buffalo '66* shows us how ephemeral life and its relation to sports truly is. A moral saga, funny, tragic, bleak. The grayness of upstate New York serves as the flip side to the bright imagery of the American sports combine. This is where the average fans, consumers all, reside. Instead of contemplating the murder of a retired football player, Billy might have instead asked the club's bartender to switch the TV overhead to a game— any game—then proceeded to pump a few rounds into the screen.

"Live your lives fully," he tells the stunned patrons as he exits. "And never bet on the Bills."

SOURCES

"Accuse Adidas of Slave Labor," Bloomberg News Service, August 19, 1998

Amdur, Neil, "Memories of 1968, With No Regrets," *New York Times,* June 14, 1998

Angell, Roger, *The Summer Game,* Penguin Books, 1990

Araton, Harvey, "Striking Back, Especially If the Shoe Fits," *New York Times,* April 12, 1998

AP Wire, "Abdul-Raul Taking His Game to Turkey," June 19, 1998

————, "White Says God Told Him to Play," April 23, 1998

Barra, Allen, "How Football Got Sacked," *New York Times Magazine,* January 12, 1997

Batard, Dan, "Prime Time Pray-er," *ESPN Magazine,* July 13, 1998

Clifford, Mark, L., Linda Himselstein and Michael Shari, "Pangs of Conscience," *Business Week,* July 29, 1996

Cushman, John, H. Jr., "Nike Pledges to End Child Labor and Apply U.S. Rules Abroad," *New York Times,* May 13, 1998

Dedman, Bill, "Where Children Play, Grown-Ups Often Brawl," *New York Times,* July 29, 1998

————, "It's a Race for the Record, but Is It Also about Race?," *New York Times,* September 20, 1998

Donnellan, Nanci (with Neal Karlen), *The Babe in Boyland,* ReganBooks, 1996

Early, Gerald, ed., *The Muhammad Ali Reader,* The Ecco Press, 1998

The ESPN Ultimate Pro Football Guide, Hyperion, 1998

Feinstein, John, *The First Coming: Tiger Woods: Master or Martyr?,* Library of Contemporary Thought, Ballantine, 1998

Galst, Liz, "In and Out," *Village Voice,* June 30, 1998

Gates, Henry Louis, Jr., "Net Worth," *The New Yorker,* June 1, 1998

Gildea, William, *Where the Game Matters Most,* Little, Brown and Co., 1997

Gitlin, Todd, "ESPN Runs the Sneaker Story That Bigfoot Networks Eschew," *New York Observer,* April 27, 1998

Gould, Lance "As the Worm Turns," *Village Voice,* August 18, 1998

Halberstam, David, *Playing for Keeps: Michael Jordan and the World He Made,* Random House, 1999

Hentoff, Nat, "The Ghosts of Andrew Young's Past," *Village Voice,* April 7, 1998

Herbert, Bob, "Fashion Statement," *New York Times,* February 15, 1998

——, "Nike Blinks," New York Times, May 21, 1998

Hill, Thomas, "Huskey HR Incites Bums in Bleachers," New York *Daily News,* April 8, 1998

Himelstein, Linda, "Nike Hasn't Scrubbed Its Image Yet," *Business Week,* July 7, 1997

Jackson, Phil (with Rick Telander), "The Last Running of the Bulls," *ESPN Magazine,* May 4, 1998

Jacobs, Andrew, "The Roots of a Religion," *New York Times,* May 31, 1998

Jensen, Jeff, "Brands, In Trouble—In Demand," *Advertising Age,* March 16, 1998

Johnson, Richard, and Jeane MacIntosh, "Nike Put the Screws to Candie's" *New York Post,* May 18, 1998

Johnson, Roy S., and Ann Harrington, "The Jordan Effect," *Fortune,* June 22, 1998

Jordan, Michael (Mark Vancil, ed.), *For the Love of the Game: My Story,* Crown, 1998

—— (with Rick Telander), "Flinch First? Not Me," *ESPN Magazine,* April 6, 1998

Kamp, David, "The NFL's Closet Case," *GQ,* January, 1998

Kawans, Howard L. (M.D.), *Why Michael Couldn't Hit, and Other Tales of the Neurology of Sports,* Avon Books, 1996

Kopay, Dave, "Dear Reggie White: You Just Don't Get It," *New York Times,* August 2, 1998

Kurtz, Howard, "CBS Reporter Creates Internal Furor Over Nike," *Washington Post,* February 11, 1998

Lee, Spike (with Ralph Wiley), *Best Seat in the House: A Basketball Memoir,* Crown Publishers, 1997

Liebling, A. J., *A Neutral Corner: Boxing Essays,* Fireside, 1990

Lipsyte, Robert, "Reflections on a Secret Life in Professional Sports," *New York Times,* September 12, 1999

Lupica, Mike, *Mad as Hell: How Sports Got Away from the Fans and How We Can Get It Back,* G. P. Putnam's Sons, 1996

Malkin, Elisabeth, "Cleanup at the *Maquiladora*," *Business Week,* July 29, 1996

Matthews, Wallace, "Sam Victimized by New Color Line," *New York Post,* September 15, 1998

——, "Hero or Pawn?," *New York Post,* September 10, 1998

——, "No Zealots Need Apply," *New York Post,* August 23, 1998

Mushnick, Phil, "Bam! Whap! I'm Rich!," *New York Post,* December 5, 1997

——, "A Dose of Reality," *New York Post,* January 11, 1998

——, "Cheapened Prayers," *New York Post,* January 25, 1998

——, "For God's Sake, Stop!," *New York Post,* May 17, 1998

——, "One Fan Took It on the Chin," *New York Post,* June 19, 1998

——, "Call in the Riot Squad," *New York Post,* September 4, 1998

Naughton, Jim, *Taking to the Air: The Rise of Michael Jordan,* Warner Books, 1992

"NBC Halts Parody of Nike Commercial," *New York Times,* February 5, 1998

Neumann, Rachel, "Straight Shooters," *Village Voice,* June 16, 1998

Nieves, Evelyn, "Pupil's Script on Workers Is Ruled Out," *New York Times,* June 26, 1997

"Nike CEO Knight Has a Very Bad Day," Bloomberg News Service, August 15, 1998

Nike Website, "Goals of Nike Marketing"

Oates, Joyce Carol, and Daniel Halpern (eds.) *Reading the Fights: The Best Writing About the Most Controversial Sport,* PrenticeHall Press, 1988

Platt, Larry, "Air Today . . . Gone Tomorrow?" *Details,* May, 1998

Plimpton, George (ed.), *The Norton Book of Sports,* W.W. Norton & Co., 1992

Reese, Lowell, "University of Kentucky Embraces Nike Despite Human Rights Record," *Kentucky Gazette,* June 17, 1997

Reno, Robert, "Invoking God as Our Quarterback in Iraq and Tampa," *Newsday,* January 29, 1991

Richmond, Peter, "Muhammad Ali in Excelsis," *GQ,* April, 1998

Rodrick, Stephen, "More Than a Game," *ESPN Magazine,* April 6, 1998

Salkin, Allen, "Hats off to Wild Creatures," *New York Post,* September 13, 1998

Sandomir, Richard, "Shoe Industry Questioning Star Power," *New York Times,* July 7, 1998

Sheed, Wilfred, "The Child of the '60s," *GQ,* April, 1998

Silver, Michael, and Don Yaeger, "Leap of Faith," *Sports Illustrated,* August 24, 1998

Smith, Chris, "God Is an .800 Hitter," *New York Times Magazine,* July 27, 1997

Solomon, Alisa, "Dousing Sparks," *Village Voice,* September 29, 1998

Stravinsky, John, "Believe," *Village Voice,* October 6, 1998

Sun Tzu, *The Art of War,* Shambhala, 1991

Susskind, Keith, *Iberian Mindfields: A Personal Trip Guide,* Bright Sky Books, 1977

Tasker, Fred, "Why Does Kathie Lee Rub Some the Wrong Way?" *The Sunday Gazzette Mail,* June 29, 1997

Tatum, Jack (with Bill Kushner), *Final Confessions of NFL Assassin Jack Tatum,* Quality Sports Publications, 1996

Vecsey, George, "Hangin' Judge Brings Peace to the Wild, Wild Frontier," *New York Times,* November 30, 1997

———, "Jim Brown Still Carries the Call for His Cause," *New York Times,* April 19, 1998

White, Reggie, March 25, 1998 Speech Transcript, Wisconsin Legislature Website

Will, George F., *Men At Work: The Craft of Baseball,* Macmillan, 1990

———, *Bunts: Curt Flood, Camden Yards, Pete Rose and Other Reflections on Baseball,* Scribner, 1998

———, "The Advisory Board That Time Forgot," *New York Post,* September 27, 1998

SOURCES

Willis, George, "Confident Stark: God's a Knick Fan," *New York Post,* May 11, 1998

Wilner, Richard, "It's The Home (Plate) Shopping Network," *New York Post,* June 25, 1998

——, "You Have To Pay To Play With Jordan," *New York Post,* August 25, 1998

Wilson, A. N., "The Good Book of Few Answers," *New York Times,* June 16, 1998

The Wisdom of Laotse, Modern Library, 1948

Wise, Mike, "Stern Talks Lockout, Questions Patriotism," *New York Times,* June 5, 1998

INDEX